UNIT 4

MELODY

Prepared for the Course Team by J. Barrie Jones

CONTENTS

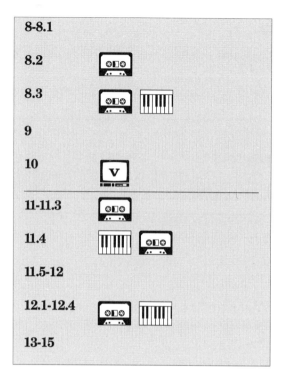

All audio items for this unit are on Audio-cassette 2 and Audio-cassette 15.

All video items for this unit can be found on Video-cassette 1.

Arts: A second-level course
Understanding Music: Elements, Techniques and Styles

UNIT 4

MELODY

UNIT 5

HARMONY I: THE CHORD

UNIT 6

MODES, SCALES AND KEYS

The Open University

The Open University, Walton Hall, Milton Keynes MK7 6AA

First published 1994

Edited, designed and typeset by the Open University.

Printed in the United Kingdom by Halstan and Co. Ltd, Amersham, Buckinghamshire.

This text forms part of an Open University second-level course. If you would like a copy of *Studying with the Open University*, please write to the Central Enquiry Service, PO Box 200, The Open University, Walton Hall, Milton Keynes, MK7 6YZ. If you have not already enrolled on the course and would like to buy this or other Open University material, please write to Open University Educational Enterprises Ltd, 12 Cofferidge Close, Stony Stratford, Milton Keynes MK11 1BY, United Kingdom.

ISBN 0 7492 1117 2

1.1

1 CONTENT AND AIMS

The topic of this unit is simply 'melody'. I shall consider various types of melody in two ways: briefly, from a historical point of view; and in more detail by asking you to hear, write, follow and play different types of melody. In so doing we shall draw together some fundamental aspects of Units 1 to 3 and (I hope) reinforce what you have already learned there.

The aims of this unit are to enable you to:

1 be aware of the musical characteristics of a range of simple melodies;

2 be able to follow easily a melody by intuitive comprehension of its musical notation;

3 be able to play various melodies on your keyboard and thus improve gradually your keyboard skills;

4 be in a position to undertake simple melodic analysis.

If the range of these aims seems formidable, it is only because any description of these necessary skills is, by its very nature, more complicated than the processes involved. Musical notation is no more difficult than the language of words, provided you are willing to spend time on the essentials at the outset. As with learning a foreign language (with which musical notation has much in common), a little practice each day produces more tangible results than a frenzied couple of hours at the week-end. I hope you will bear this in mind, not just in this unit, but throughout the course.

You will need Audio-cassette 2 for this unit. You should have pencil, manuscript paper and an eraser to hand, as well as easy access to your keyboard and video equipment. You will also need to refer to your scores of the Beethoven Fifth Symphony, the Tchaikovsky *Serenade for Strings* and Schubert's Octet. The unit breaks off after Sections 6 and 9 in order to offer some teaching through video. The music examples on video appear in Sections 7 and 10, which contain video notes.

At times in this unit I will have to introduce the names of composers, genres, historical periods and so on which have not been explained either here or in the preceding units. For the moment I must ask you to take these on trust. They will be covered more fully later in the course.

2 MELODY: PAST AND PRESENT

2.1 SOME DEFINITIONS

I have said that the topic of this unit is melody, but I have not defined what the word 'melody' means. For the moment, we can say that rhythm and pitch in combination produce what is known as **melody**. A more familiar and everyday term for this is *tune*. As with so many apparently simple terms, any definition is unlikely to be all-embracing or appropriate for all musical contexts. Here is one brief explanation of melody:

> In the most general sense, a coherent succession of pitches.
>
> (H. S. Powers, *New Harvard Dictionary of Music*, p. 481)

Powers then compares and contrasts the phenomenon of melody with that of harmony, rather as you did with Schubert's theme that you heard in the Course Introduction. *The New Grove* devotes nine pages to the subject of melody; the opening sentence attempts first to define the term as follows:

> Melody, defined as pitched sounds arranged in musical time in accordance with given cultural conventions and constraints, represents a universal human phenomenon traceable to prehistoric times …
>
> (A. L. Ringer, *The New Grove*, Vol. 12, p. 118)

Neither of these definitions conveys the supreme importance that melody has for the majority of composers. And, for many people, melody is the most important, perhaps the only, component when evaluating music. One of the aims of this course will be to show that, as a rule, melody is merely one of many different aspects that must be considered when examining a piece of music. But this unit will concentrate on melody.

2.2 ATTITUDES

There are certain pieces of music where, if the melody itself fails, the piece fails as a whole. For example, the waltzes of Johann Strauss (1825–99) are most memorable for their melodic content, despite their frequently colourful orchestral effects and infectious rhythmic lilt. Some twentieth-century popular songs belong to the same category. On the other hand, the appeal of 1950s rock-and-roll is primarily rhythmic; and a full appreciation of some pre-World War 2 Broadway hits, as well as the later shows by Stephen Sondheim (*b*.1930), depends on the recognition of a sometimes quite sophisticated harmonic vocabulary.

A number of great musical masterpieces of the past cannot be evaluated by an examination of the initial melody. A fugue by J. S. Bach is a good example of a piece where the initial idea is merely a starting point for the composer's ingenuity, technical skill and constructional abilities. It is not so much the initial presentation of a melody that is important, but what happens to it later. The two greatest composers of the late-eighteenth century, Haydn and Mozart, differed from each other in several respects but nowhere more so than in the way they approached the melodic aspect of composition. It is generally fair to say that Haydn's greatest gift lay in the way in which he manipulated his musical material, whereas Mozart's strength lay in the profusion, immediate attractiveness and balanced construction of his melodies. In rather different ways, the same comparison is appropriate for Beethoven and Schubert respectively. Although generalizations can be dangerous oversimplifications, they sometimes provide a useful starting point – and may be qualified subsequently.

2.3 POLYPHONY AND CANON

In this subsection, I want to consider briefly two genres of composition that exploit the possibilities of melodic combination. The first is a type of composition, found at its most imposing in the sixteenth century, whereby several lines of melody are heard simultaneously. The total impression is one of an interweaving of sinuous melodic strands. Such writing is known as **polyphony** ('many sounds' in Greek) and found its purest expression in the polyphonic mass[1] of sixteenth-century Italy. It is one of nature's paradoxes that the human ear can readily distinguish four or even more simultaneous melodic lines, but finds intolerable as few as two human voices speaking at the same time. Thus the power of music over speech. On Audio-cassette 2 you can hear, as Item 1, the *Kyrie eleison* (Lord, have mercy) from Palestrina's *Missa Aeterna Christi Munera* (Mass 'The perpetual gifts of Christ'), a short movement of a little over two minutes' length and written for four voices. Try to hear how each voice keeps its own shapely line and yet blends harmoniously with its fellows.

 LISTEN NOW TO ITEM 1.

---

[1]   The Eucharist ritual, commemorating the life and death of Christ. The main form is the High (or Solemn) Mass; two others are the Requiem Mass (for the Dead) and the *Missa Brevis* (a shortened form of the High Mass).

The second musical genre, the canon, is one where polyphony is created by having a single tune sung by several voices, which enter in turn in strict imitation. *Three Blind Mice* and *Tallis's Canon* are well-known examples. A second, third or even fourth part can enter by imitation at specified points in the music. Such pieces are more akin to riddles or puzzles than to what we normally think of as musical compositions, and the melody, perhaps even the music itself, takes a secondary position to the intellectual skill of the composer. Canons were comparatively frequent in the Mediaeval and Renaissance periods (which musicians tend to date respectively as from *c.*1000 to *c.*1450, and from *c.*1450 and *c.*1600).

Figure 1 illustrates a musical canon by John Bull (1562/3–1628) in the form of a musical puzzle. The music has to be 'discovered' by putting into effect a set of musical rules. Thankfully, modern musical notation is not so complex!

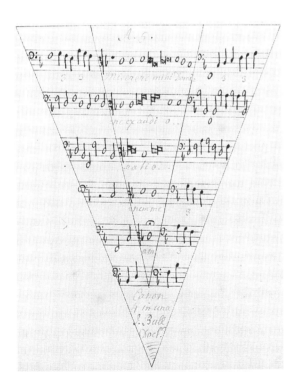

Figure 1   John Bull's 'Canon 4 in una' ('Canon 4 in one') from an eighteenth-century manuscript ascribed to Elway Bevin. British Library Manuscript.

3   HISTORICAL PERSPECTIVES

3.1   ANCIENT GREECE

To the ancient Greeks, music was frequently a handmaid of drama. In fact, their word *musike* ('of the Muses') included by implication what we should describe as music, poetry, drama and astrology. In whatever form we should describe it, music was certainly important to the Greeks, who regarded differing aspects of it as conducive to manliness, as an encouragement to war-like fervour, as pleasing to the senses and so on. In Unit 3 Section 4 you played the scale of C major. In ancient Greece, scales were known as *modes*, a term in regular use until *c.*1600 and later. We know very little of the sort of music written by the Greeks, and such fragments as survive date from a relatively late period. The conventional view until comparatively recently was that harmony, as we understand it, did not exist; in other words, ancient Greek music consisted of single lines of melody, perhaps with occasional octave doublings.[2] The music had perforce to be entirely subservient to the accompanying poetry, a situation also obtaining later in many of the earliest operas written in Florence around 1600. Nevertheless, it seems almost inconceivable that a type of harmony, however simple, did not exist in some form in ancient Greece.

3.2   STRUCTURES

In literature, both small- and large-scale works have survived over a long period of time. The vast historical and narrative epics of Homer and Virgil, the exquisite miniature poems of Ovid, and many other substantial and small-scale works survive from both the Homeric age and that of Classical Greece and Rome. Western music presumably used small-scale structures as far back as Classical antiquity, but, in contrast to literature, large-scale structures have developed only gradually and very much more recently. Because of music's early dependence on the human voice and on instruments of limited power and range, it is scarcely surprising that the smaller musical structures were the first to be cultivated. Instrumental music was conceived originally as an accompaniment to dance or song, and only very slowly did it emancipate itself to emerge as a viable force in its own right. One might say that music as such hardly existed as an autonomous practice, in the sense we think of now, before the later Middle Ages.

[2]   'Octave doubling' means that a note (or series of notes) sounds simultaneously with its higher (or lower) octave.

3.3 PLAINSONG

Plainsong (or **plainchant**) refers to that vast body of pure, unaccompanied, sacred melodies as developed by the early Christian Church. They form the earliest European melodies to survive complete and are still in regular use. And because they are single lines of melody they are *monodic*, a term you may remember from Unit 2, Section 10.3. (Palestrina used the plainsong *Aeterna Christi Munera* as the basis for his Mass of that title, whose *Kyrie* you have just heard.) These melodies were a natural development of the intoning of liturgical words; many of these tunes date from the seventh, eighth and ninth centuries. A few are closer in date to some of the music of ancient Greece than to that of our own day. The reasons for their continued survival are not difficult to discover: to the Roman Catholic Church, plainsong represented the mystical union between God and mankind, and many of these melodies are of very great beauty. Each sacred text possessed its own plainchant, to be sung without accompaniment and usually with no definitely measured rhythms. To quote from one dictionary:

> Its groupings of notes have, however, a strongly rhythmic character, but it resembles the free rhythm of prose, whereas that of measured music is comparable to the rhythm of verse.

(E. Blom, *New Everyman*, p. 570)

You may perhaps have heard recordings of the monks at the Benedictine Abbey at Solesmes, between Angers and Le Mans in western France. In fact, plainsong was not always sung non-metrically ('the free rhythm of prose'), but for our purposes the above definition is more than sufficient. Because the 'rhythm' of the words themselves dictated that of the tune, there was no need to show such rhythm in the notation, save to indicate how many notes were to be sung to a syllable. For this, special signs were employed, known as *ligatures*. You saw some of these in Figures 4 and 7 of Unit 3.

Here is a plainsong melody which you will be studying later in the unit, but you may perhaps like to listen to it now. It is Item 2 on the audio-cassette.

Example 1   Bellator armis inclitus

   LISTEN NOW TO ITEM 2.

There are a number of points that I need to make in discussing this melody, but I want to leave them until a little later in this unit.

3.4 CONCLUSIONS

We have seen that Greek music was probably monodic, that plainsong too was monodic and rhythmically free, that in the Middle Ages there were complex canons, and that in the Middle Ages and Renaissance there were polyphonic masses. Later music, however, sometimes concentrates on harmony and rhythm, rather than melody itself. Thus the history of melody is not a gradual evolution from the simple to the complex; rather, each era has developed its own complexities in the way it uses melody. Were an ancient Greek melody of 2000 BC miraculously to come to light, it is possible that its structure would be far more complicated than that of many present-day pop songs. Many Mediaeval tunes are extremely elaborate compared with, say, melodies by Wagner and Beethoven. However, for the next section I want to return to simple melodies.

4   SOME PRACTICAL WORK (I)

4.1 SIMPLE TUNES

I want now to turn your attention to the reading, writing and playing of some simple tunes, mostly folk-songs. I shall discuss the historical aspects of folk-song in Section 11. In the meantime you will still need Audio-cassette 2 to hand so that you can hear and follow the examples. I shall play them on the piano and you can check these against your own efforts on the keyboard.

4.2 SUO-GÂN

You will remember from Unit 3, Section 4, that you played on your keyboard a series of notes from middle C up to the C one octave higher. Including the first C, there were seven white notes before you reached the next C. Some white notes had black notes between, others did not. These seven notes are thus not equidistant from each other: C to D, for example, is a bigger 'step' than from E to F. I hope you remember from Section 5 of Unit 3 that this smallest possible step (or interval) on your keyboard is a *semitone*. The two white notes without an intervening black one (B and C as well as E and F) are an interval of a semitone apart, as indeed are any black note and its immediately adjacent white neighbour. The bigger white-note steps (C to D, D to E, etc.) are intervals of a *tone*: one tone is equal to two semitones. I shall go into more detail on this in Unit 6, but let us stop there for the moment. If you want to play a C major scale, *try it again now, starting on middle C and going up to the C one octave higher*. (Refer back to the video notes in Section 9 of Unit 2 if you need to remind yourself where middle C is.)

 PLAY.

You have already practised some five-note exercises in the video work in Unit 3, so you should have little trouble with the following tune. It uses only the first three notes of the scale, which you can play using the thumb and first two fingers of the right hand. It is the Welsh folk-song *Suo-Gân* (pronounced approximately *Seeoh-Gaaan*). Obviously, we shall be using white notes only. The tune exists in more than one form, but we are using the simplest and probably the oldest form of the tune. First the two verses are sung, and since the singer is a man, the music will sound one octave lower than in the notation here. Then you will hear me playing one verse on the piano. These are Items 3 and 3(a).

Example 2   Suo-Gân

 LISTEN NOW TO ITEMS 3 AND 3(a).

The words are:

Verse 1

Winter creeps,
Nature sleeps;
Birds are gone,
Flowers are none,
Fields are bare,
Cold the air;
Leaves are shed,
All seems dead.

Verse 2

But the spring
Soon will bring
Early buds
To the woods.
Lambs will play
All the day;
Nought but green
Will be seen.

Exercises

 Try to clap the rhythm of *Suo-Gân*, making sure that your two quavers fit exactly into one crotchet. Then, try to play this melody on your keyboard, starting with the thumb of your right hand on the first note. Listen to it again on the cassette. Then play it again on the keyboard.

When you have this fluently under your fingertips, try it starting with your middle finger. This practice will be helpful later when you progress to melodies with more notes, and need to use all your fingers.

Example 3 gives the tune an octave higher. Play it on your keyboard several times, starting with the thumb and then with your middle finger.

Example 3

Try playing the tune with your left hand. Again, try it in two ways: starting with your little finger, and then using your middle one. Example 4 shows the tune in the bass clef.

Example 4

Finally, try copying out this tune once or twice to give yourself some writing practice. You will probably want to refer to Sections 3 and 6 of Unit 3 if your writing skills have become a little rusty.

4.3 *ROSIE'S SKIRT*

As you no doubt feel by now, such a tune as *Suo-Gân* is somewhat limited as pure melody. In many folk-songs the accompanying words are at least as important as the tune, and in *Suo-Gân* are probably more so. Let's therefore turn to a more interesting tune, which adds the fourth and fifth notes of the scale to the three you have just used. Each note will therefore fit nicely beneath each digit of your hand. You will notice that this melody, as one might expect from its greater range, is somewhat longer than *Suo-Gân*. It is a folk tune from Czechoslovakia, called (in translation) *Rosie's Skirt*. This time, in accordance with convention, I have placed the words underneath the melody. Once again, you will hear the tune with its words, and then it will be played a second time on the piano: these are Items 4 and 4(a) respectively.

Example 5

LISTEN NOW TO ITEMS 4 AND 4(a).

Exercise

Play this melody at your keyboard and try playing it an octave higher and an octave lower. Remember always to start with the thumb, since in this tune we need a digit for each different pitch.

PLAY EXAMPLE 5.

If you have time, practise writing the melody in both treble and bass clefs. If you want to try playing this tune with your left hand, remember to start with your little finger!

5 CADENCES

As a short break from these exercises, I want to draw your attention to an important term which will be reintroduced in Unit 6, and frequently thereafter. The word is cadence, from the Latin *cadere*, to fall. It can be defined as a logical ending to a phrase or movement based on certain accepted melodic and harmonic formulae. A convenient analogy exists here between music and language. A cadence is really a type of musical punctuation: full stop, colon, etc. Cadences are much easier to hear and to see in the score when there is a bass part, since the cadential formula is frequently indicated by the bass line. You will be adding a bass line to *Rosie's Skirt* later in the course.

In Example 6 I have added a bracket to the fourth bar of *Rosie's Skirt*. When you play and hear this, can you sense a 'falling feeling' in the music at bar 4 where I have placed a bracket?

Example 6

Ro - sie has a new skirt, it's ve - ry big and lum - py.

 PLAY EXAMPLE 6 NOW.

This feeling is due partly to the fact that we have reached the end of a 4-bar 'unit' and partly because the melody has finally returned to the home note, C. The phrase is obviously not satisfactory as a complete piece, but it certainly makes more sense musically than it would if we were to stop the music after bar 2. (Try playing bars 1–2 and stopping!). At this point we have left the home note far behind. There is a cadence in bar 4, where the home note is regained. There are different types of cadence, and the one here is known as a **'perfect' cadence**. It is the equivalent of a full stop in language. Think of cadences, for the moment, as places where a melody comes to a very brief resting spot. I will not go into more details about cadences here; the concept will be taken up later in the course.

6 SOME PRACTICAL WORK (II)

6.1 ACCIDENTALS (SHARPS)

Let us return to *Suo-Gân*, with which I hope you are now reasonably familiar.

Example 7 Suo-Gân

Exercise 1

First, write out *Suo-Gân*, but this time starting on the G above middle C:

Remember you have to reproduce the melodic shape at the higher pitch. (You may remember from Section 6.3 of Unit 3 that this activity is known as *transposition*.) Then play it on your keyboard. I hope you feel that the melody sounds 'correct'. Check your answer with the one at the end of the unit.

 PLAY YOUR TRANSPOSITION.

Now try playing this melody beginning one step up from middle C, i.e. from the note D:

Remember, as always, to start this tune with your thumb.

 PLAY.

Do you feel that there is something 'wrong' with the third note? If not, can you see on your keyboard that there is no black note between the E and the F? There was such a black note between the D and the E, when you played this tune starting on C. The third note of *Suo-Gân* must be a whole tone distant from the second, not a half (or semi) tone. Try playing the first of the group of three black notes, lying just to the right of the note F, as your third note:

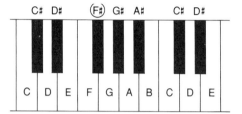

Figure 2

 PLAY.

Did you feel that sounded better than the first time? For your third note you played F sharp rather than F. In fact, you did just the same with *Frère Jacques* in Unit 3, Section 5. I hope you can recall from this section that the musical symbol we use to indicate this is a ♯ which is placed just before the note we need to sharpen – or raise by half-a-tone, because, as you remember, two semitones are equal to one tone.

Exercise 2

Now write out *Suo-Gân* starting on the note D, and placing this sharp against each F. The answer is at the end of the unit. Now try doing the same for *Rosie's Skirt*. Starting on D, write out the tune yourself, placing a ♯ against each F. Again, the answer is at the end of the unit. Now try it in the bass clef, starting on the middle line of the stave. Check what you have written with the answer at the end of the unit.

Perhaps you might care to play Examples 33 and 34 in the answer to Exercise 2 simultaneously (i.e. in octaves). Read from *either* Example 33 *or* Example 34 but try using both hands for the one example.

 PLAY.

6.2 KEY SIGNATURES

You may be wondering whether every black note on the keyboard needs an accompanying ♯ (or ♭) whenever it appears in a written piece of music. And would this not be somewhat cumbersome? In fact, it was the standard practice in certain types of music written before *c.*1600, in as much as one can refer to any 'standard practice' before this date. It was especially the preferred notational convention in keyboard music. Only when the recurring sharps became too numerous did someone hit on the idea of a **key signature**, where the necessary symbols could be written just once per stave at the very beginning of each line of music. Key signatures existed before 1600, but on a (to us) none-too-logical basis. Now take a quick look at the start of the second movement of Tchaikovsky's *Serenade for Strings* in your miniature score. Just before the time signature of ¾ (three crotchets to the bar, of course) you can see the single ♯, signifying that all the Fs in the piece are to be raised by one semitone, unless there are instructions to the contrary in the music itself. No doubt all this may seem a little confusing, but it will become clear before too long. For the moment, keep the business of key signatures at the back of your mind. I shall discuss keys and their signatures in much more detail in Unit 6.

6.3 ACCIDENTALS (FLATS)

And what about the ♭ sign? If you look at your copy of the miniature score, you will see that there are three of them at the start of Beethoven's Fifth Symphony and four, no less, at the opening of the last movement of Schubert's Octet. (Look back at Section 5.2 in Unit 3 if you need to remind yourself about the ♭ sign.) Let us see how we can introduce one into *Rosie's Skirt*. If you need to remind yourself of this tune, play it a few times in the various ways I suggested in Section 4.3. Otherwise, try playing this tune starting from the F above middle C. The first phrase (see Example 8) will somehow sound wrong to you (I hope!), in that the fourth note seems strange if you play it as the 'white' note.

Example 8

PLAY.

As with *Suo-Gân* there is a problem, but now it is with the fourth note. When you start on C, the third and fourth notes are absolutely adjacent, i.e. no black note separates them. This is not the case when you commence on the note F: the white notes A and B are separated by one black note, and it is this black note that is needed to create the smallest step between the third and fourth notes. A semitone, in fact. The white note, B, is a semitone too high and must be lowered (or flattened) by one semitone, so that our original pattern of large and small steps can be preserved. To lower a written note by a semitone we place a ♭ in front of it, and when playing it, we play the adjacent black note to the left. Here, then, is *Rosie's Skirt* complete, starting on F and including all the flats we need for this tune.

Example 9

Exercises

Play this several times, remembering to start with your thumb, of course, and try playing it an octave lower too. Then write the tune out in treble and bass clefs to give yourself some writing practice. Persevere until your writing and playing are reasonably fluent. You may find this quite a slow process, or you might pick it up fairly easily. Remember: frequent brief practices are more effective than the occasional tedious hour.

 PLAY.

You should now turn to Unit 4, Video Section 1, for my discussion of melodic range and intervals.

7 MELODIC RANGE AND INTERVALS

 **VIDEO NOTES
UNIT 4, VIDEO SECTION 1**

Introduction

This video section deals with two separate concepts: melodic range and intervals.

You will need your keyboard and audio-cassette player.

Before the video section

Familiarize yourself with Video Example 1, which is the French tune *Au Clair de la lune* (In the Silver Moonlight). The first four bars are rather similar to the equivalent bars of *Suo-Gân*. It is played for you on the audio-cassette as Item 5.

 LISTEN NOW TO ITEM 5.

Try playing it on your keyboard and writing it out.

  NOW WATCH THE VIDEO SECTION. YOU WILL ALSO NEED YOUR KEYBOARD AND AUDIO-CASSETTE PLAYER.

During the video section

Melodic range

The video section shows you the fingering to use for *Au Clair de la lune*. You might like to add the fingerings to Video Example 1.[3]

Video Example 1   Au Clair de la lune

Video Example 2   Suo-Gân

When you are first asked to stop the tape, you should play Video Example 1. Remember to begin with your middle finger on G, and watch out for the black note in bar 11.

The second time you are asked to stop the tape you should play *Au Clair de la lune* again, but starting on F and on C. These versions will not use any black notes. You can play them by following the fingering you used for Video Example 1.

The video section continues directly to the concept of intervals, but you

[3] You might spot that the notation of *Au Clair de la lune* and *Suo-Gân* in the video section doesn't follow the 'rule' outlined in the footnote in Unit 3, Section 3.3, for deciding the stem direction of notes on the middle stave-line.

might like to take a break before watching it.

Intervals

Video Example 3   *Scale of C major*

The third time you are asked to stop the tape you should play Video Examples 4 and 5.

Video Example 4   *Intervals from middle C*

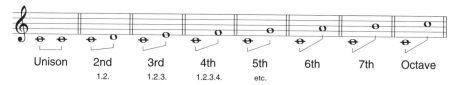

Video Example 5   *Simultaneously sounding intervals (two-part chords)*

You can hear the intervals in Video Examples 4 and 5 played as Items 6 and 7 on the audio-cassette. Listen for the characteristic sound of each interval, and then try playing them on the keyboard yourself.

    LISTEN TO ITEMS 6 AND 7.

Summary

When calculating intervals, remember to include the lower note as 1. The interval from C to D is a second; from C to E a third, etc. When played together, some intervals are consonant, others dissonant.

Remember the word *cadence*, which will figure a great deal in the course before too long.

7.1 INTERVALS

We've just been talking about intervals and their construction on the video. Let's see whether you can recall one of the important matters I raised there.

Drawing on what we've just done, can you remember the rule we formulated for the calculation of the distance between two notes?

 PAUSE AND THINK.

You have to count the number of notes from the lower to the higher note, including both the notes in your calculations. Remember, too, that the inclusive-count rule applies for both the simultaneous and the successive sounding of two notes. Try to recognize both the sound and the notational appearance of all the intervals from seconds to sevenths. To help you learn to do this, I'm going to ask you to play examples of various intervals and then describe them as thirds, fifths or whatever.

Example 10 gives the intervals. They all have C as their lower note.

Example 10

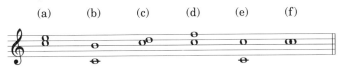

 **PLAY THE INTERVALS IN EXAMPLE 10.**

LISTEN TO ITEM 8, IN WHICH I PLAY THE INTERVALS.

Exercise 3

Name the intervals in Example 10. Don't forget to count the lower note as 1. The answers are at the end of the unit.

If you got these wrong, look at Video Section 1 and the notes again. If you got the unison correct, well done, since your ear is obviously quite discriminating.

Finally, I'd like to return to the plainsong melody which I gave earlier as Example 1. I have reproduced it below as Example 11, using minims and crotchets rather than the stemless noteheads of Example 1.

Example 11   Bellator armis inclitus

It's a tune of great beauty and is, you notice, contained within an octave. As I remarked in Section 3, rhythmic notation is conventionally regarded as fluid in plainsong, so I have not attempted to force the tune into regular metrical bars. The four double bar lines mark merely the end of each musical line. Remember that this tune occurs in its plainsong version earlier in the audio-cassette as Item 2, but I'll play it on the piano for you first, and then the plainsong version will follow.

LISTEN NOW TO ITEMS 9 AND 9(a).

Exercise 4

(a) Name the bracketed intervals marked a, b, c and d.

(b) Look at and play, if you can, the four lines of the tune. Can you spot any relationships or musical connections between them?

The answers are given at the end of the unit.

8 MELODIC ANALYSIS

8.1 PHRASE STRUCTURE (I)

The fact that our plainsong, quoted in Examples 1 and 11, begins and ends with the same music while enclosing different material within, demonstrates a fundamental law in the construction of melodies and, by extension, in the building-up of musical paragraphs, sections and whole movements. This is the need for some form of repetition or return to an initial statement, so as to satisfy what seems to be an innate human desire for balance and symmetry. Very little music continues by merely stringing one new section of music after another. One of the most frequent and satisfying structures consists of a first section, a contrasting section and a return to the initial section. This structure is known as either ABA, or **ternary form**. Although its B section subsumes two phrases of different music, our plainsong falls into this category. This design is found in much later music, such as many nineteenth-century piano pieces and the eighteenth-century minuet. It also became a very common pattern in European folk-song.

On the cassette I used the words 'musical line' in referring to the four plainsong phrases. I should perhaps have said 'musical phrase'. In Example 12 you will see that I have added curved lines below the music. Unit 3 introduced you to phrase marks, and each curve often covers one *phrase*. As you remember, there are often performance implications in phrase marks, since a *legato* style is frequently appropriate. In music, the meaning of the term 'phrase' is analogous to its literary meaning. That is, one 'breathes' at the phrase endings. In fact, phrases sound as though they have endings because they have *cadences*. (Re-read Section 5 if you need to.) A phrase is a short section of music which makes musical sense in itself, but usually requires a number of others to form a meaningful 'sentence'. A complete tune might consist of, say, a 16-bar sentence, subdivided into 4 four-bar phrases. Actually there are many other possible patterns. Let us therefore look at the phrase structures of the three melodies we have studied so far.

8.2 SOME ALTERNATIVES

Items 10 and 10(a) on the audio-cassette are *Suo-Gân* in its sung version of two verses (i.e. Example 12 is sung twice), then played on the piano.

Example 12

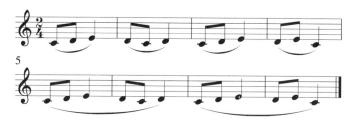

 LISTEN NOW TO ITEMS 10 AND 10(a).

This tune, apparently so simple, can be analysed into phrases in more than one way. For example, you might regard bar 1 as a basic unit and a single phrase in its own right; it is actually repeated in bar 3. Bars 2 and 4 are different both from bar 1 and from each other. Schematically, therefore, the first four bars could then be analysed as ABAC. There is here a satisfying contrast between old and new material.

On the other hand, especially if one imagines a brisker tempo, the first two bars can be conceived as one unit, and similarly bars 3–4. As you can see, the different phrase marks in bars 5–8 above reflect this alternative. Such a probability is more likely, especially since bars 5–8 are identical to bars 1–4. Thus, the whole tune would be represented schematically as ABAB, and diagrammatically by Figure 3.

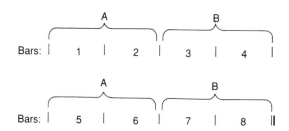

Figure 3

I should also point out that the B section is itself related to A, because their first bars are identical.

You can see, therefore, that even a simple tune such as *Suo-Gân* needs to be examined with some care if its structure is to be analysed successfully. (I should add here that when we analyse more extensive movements by composers such as Beethoven or Brahms, we do not make use of a whole alphabet of letters. In these cases, several musical phrases are subsumed into paragraphs of music, and there may be many of these in a section then represented by a single letter. Many Romantic piano pieces use a simple ABA ternary structure, but each of those letters will include a number of musical phrases.)

8.3 PHRASE STRUCTURE (II)

In the following two exercises I will ask you to analyse the phrase structuring of the other two songs we have met, *Rosie's Skirt* and *Au Clair de la lune*.

Exercise 5

Example 13 shows *Rosie's Skirt* with the phrases marked. You can hear it sung and played as Items 11 and 11(a) on the audio-cassette. Use letters (A, B, C etc.) to represent schematically the phrase structure of the tune. The answer is at the end of the unit.

 LISTEN TO ITEMS 11 AND 11(a).

Example 13

Discussion

You probably noticed that the overall feeling is that of an ABA ternary scheme, where the three sections correspond to bars 1–8, 9–16 and 17–20. AABBA is technically correct. Many people would prefer ABA as a convenient shortened form. Note that not all sections with the same letter need be exactly the same length. (Compare bars 1–8 and 17–20.)

Exercise 6

Example 14 is *Au Clair de la lune*, again with the phrases marked. It is sung and played in Items 12 and 12(a). Describe the phrase structure schematically, using A, B, C etc. The answer is at the end of the unit.

 LISTEN TO ITEMS 12 AND 12(a).

Example 14

Discussion

I hope you found both of these exercises reasonably straightforward. If you had any difficulties, listen carefully once again to the audio-cassette items, following the music. Try playing them yourself on the keyboard. By the way, you may perhaps have divided *Au Clair de la lune* into 2-bar phrases, on the grounds that the rhythmic pattern is repeated. The resulting proliferation of letters would be an unlikely analysis in so short a tune. Don't worry too much if you treated the melody in this way, but in general always aim for the simplest possible analysis, where appropriate.

Although *Au Clair de la lune* may not have given you many problems, I admit that the B section of *Rosie's Skirt* might well have presented you with various choices. Is bar 9 a single unit, repeated immediately in bar 10, and then slightly varied in bar 11, then repeated in bar 12? If so, you would then have to consider for bars 9–12 the scheme BBB'B' where the ' signifies a varied repetition of the basic material. (You could call it *variation* or *development*, but these terms need to be used with care, as they are also used in other musical contexts.) This literal treatment of B is theoretically possible, but it is so fussy when compared with that of A that I prefer either of the two versions I suggested for that melody. When in doubt, choose simplicity rather than complexity.

These varied possibilities are by no means unique to this kind of analysis; indeed, you will find that any prolonged study of music is frequently a curious mixture of science and a range of more nebulous philosophical considerations. Music is both a science and an art. It is this unique combination which gives music its particular place in a long and distinguished history of human achievement.

9   PATTERN AND EMOTION

One of music's numerous definitions is that of an ordered succession of sounds across a spectrum of time. And within that time spectrum, whether it be the vast structure of a Wagner opera, a brief Chopin prelude or *Suo-Gân*, there will be peaks and troughs, tensions and resolutions, approaches to climaxes and the consequences of those climaxes. There is an infinite number of possible patterns – indeed every piece will have its own pattern – although the number of different 'emotional journeys' is relatively small.

For example, one scheme frequently found in some late-eighteenth- and much nineteenth-century music is the questing, often questioning, opening which gradually progresses through to a triumphant end: from darkness to light, if you prefer. Beethoven's Fifth Symphony, although beginning questioningly rather than darkly, certainly ends in a blaze of triumph. On the other hand, some nineteenth-century pieces begin in a mood of calm, reach a climax perhaps three-quarters of the way through, then return to the mood of the opening. Numerous Romantic piano pieces utilize this pattern. Such structures manipulate these various tensions and resolutions on a large scale so as to give the piece its specific emotional character. I now want to turn to one particular technical point on a small-scale level: antecedent and consequent. You should therefore now turn to your second section of video before proceeding any further with this unit. As before, the music examples on the video are reproduced in Section 10 below.

10   ANTECEDENT AND CONSEQUENT

 VIDEO NOTES
UNIT 4, VIDEO SECTION 2

Introduction

The terms antecedent and consequent essentially mean tension and resolution; question and answer are also an appropriate equivalent.

NOW WATCH THE VIDEO SECTION.

During the video section

You are asked a question on Video Example 13. At the appropriate instruction to stop the tape, look ahead to Video Example 13 and try to answer the following question: Remembering what you have learnt about antecedent and consequent, how would you describe the two phrases of Video Example 13, and why?

Examples played during the video section

Video Example 6   Suo-Gân

Video Example 7   Twinkle, Twinkle, *first phrase, antecedent*

Video Example 8   Twinkle, Twinkle, *second phrase, consequent*

Video Example 9   The British Grenadiers, *first phrase, antecedent*

Video Example 10   The British Grenadiers, *second phrase, consequent*

Video Example 11, the opening of Mozart's Fourth Violin Concerto, is rather neutral in its effect.

Video Example 11   *Opening of Mozart's Fourth Violin Concerto*

And with the first eight bars of *Pop! Goes the Weasel* (Video Example 12) the surprise comes in bar 7. The three asterisks show the tune returning continually to the note C. The ? indicates the sudden surprise.

Video Example 12   Pop! Goes the Weasel

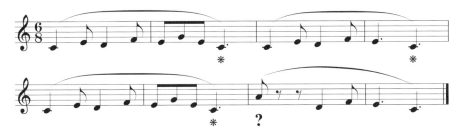

Using the terms 'antecedent' and 'consequent', how would you describe the two phrases of Video Example 13, and why? This question is answered in the video section.

Video Example 13   *Opening of Haydn's* Emperor's Hymn

Summary

The basis of question and answer in melody is to balance an incomplete-sounding phrase with one that completes it. Look at the above examples to see how this applies. The fifth note of the scale (G in a scale starting on C) is called the **dominant**. It has a particularly strong relationship to the home note: in this case C. And this home note, the first note of the scale we are using, is known as the **tonic**. Although the dominant is not the only note to suggest a feeling of incompleteness, it is perhaps the one which gives the strongest feeling of a need to return there because of that strong pull towards the tonic. *Twinkle, Twinkle Little Star* is a clear example of this feeling. Put in more technical language, when tonic moves to dominant, some form of *tension* (antecedent) is established which must, eventually, lead to a *resolution* (consequent) of that tension.

There are different levels of antecedence and consequence. For instance, a phrase which is an antecedent might itself be analysable into antecedent and consequent parts.

From now on I shall use the words tonic and dominant to refer to the first and fifth degrees of the scale.

Exercise

Add the labels 'antecedent' and 'consequent', where appropriate, to *Au Clair de la lune* (Example 14).

Answer

Bars

1–2 = Antecedent

3–4 = Consequent

5–6 = Antecedent

7–8 = Consequent

9–10 = Antecedent

11–12 = Consequent

13–14 = Antecedent

15–16 = Consequent

Discussion

Needless to say, not all tunes lend themselves to so symmetrical and obvious a solution! And indeed the consequent in bars 11–12 could be regarded as an antecedent. You may perhaps have already noticed that the last note of bar 12 is the *dominant*: in other words it is posing a question. This ambiguity is explained by the fact that this

phrase is no longer based on the home note, G, but has moved away on to a different level (or home note). The tune has changed key, or **modulated**. Do not worry about this now; accept this apparent inconsistency, since the concept of modulation will be taken up later in the course.

11 FOLK-SONGS AND TRADITIONAL SONGS

11.1 SOME DEFINITIONS

We have been studying a number of folk-songs in this unit. What exactly is a folk-song? The first edition of a famous musical dictionary offered a definition that is now regarded as somewhat old-fashioned and one that has been attacked by many folklorists. It runs as follows:

> The musical repertory and tradition of communities, as opposed to art music which is the artistic expression of musically trained individuals. It develops anonymously, usually among the 'lower classes', together with artless poems dealing with the various phases of daily life: working songs, love songs, cradle songs, drinking songs, patriotic songs, dancing songs, mourning songs, narrative and epic songs, etc.
>
> (W. Apel, *Harvard Dictionary of Music*, p. 274)

Without expressly saying so, this definition implies that folk-songs were written by anonymous and untrained musical amateurs, and were handed down orally from generation to generation. (This was not always the case.) Many familiar British songs date from the eighteenth century, although a surprising number come from the sixteenth. *The New Grove* introduces a more international perspective in its introductory definition:

> The notion that there is such a thing as 'folk music' as distinct from other kinds of music is widespread in Europe and America. Elsewhere the need for such a concept is felt less strongly, and in some parts of the world, especially in Africa, people do not make such distinctions.
>
> (K. P. Wachsmann, *The New Grove*, Vol. 6, p. 693)

11.2 SOME HISTORICAL BACKGROUND

An upsurge of interest in folk-songs was widespread in some European countries during the second half of the eighteenth century, and particularly from the 1770s onwards. There were frequent publications of folk-songs, such as the collections of *Volkslieder* (Folk-songs) in 1778–9 by the German philosopher and theologian Johann Herder (1744–1803) and a similar collection of 80 Russian folk-songs by Vasiliy Trutovsky (*c.*1740–1810), published at various times between 1776 and 1795. This interest continued throughout the nineteenth century. The rise of musical nationalism, especially as manifested in Eastern Europe after *c.*1850, encompassed such matters as the increasing interest in folk-song and frequently in the collecting of them, along with the quotation and assimilation of folk-songs in art music. For the music historian, such interrelationships between folk and art point to the difficulty in defining what a true folk-song really is. Even specialists are often unable to distinguish between genuine folk-songs and reasonably sophisticated imitations of them by trained, albeit sometimes anonymous, composers. (In Britain such imitations have become known as traditional songs.) Herder's collections influenced the song writing of, and perhaps the melodic casts of some instrumental music by, both Schumann and Brahms.[4] And though it is rather more sophisticated and instrumental in character than a true folk-song, the melody from Schubert's Octet that you heard at the beginning of the course seems – to the modern listener at least – to contain something of the character of a (good) folk-song.

11.3 FOLK OR TRADITIONAL: IS THERE A DIFFERENCE?

Traditional song is often described as 'sophisticated', implying that a folk-song was unsophisticated and 'simple'. In fact, Hungarian folk-songs and Irish Gaelic ballads can be surprisingly complex rhythmically. On the other hand, many 'traditional' tunes have been absorbed into the folk repertory and as a result their style became very influential on folk musicians. It is, in fact, dangerous to try to establish musical distinctions between folk and traditional tunes. Essentially, the two categories interpenetrate stylistically: many tunes classed as folk tunes seem to modulate (e.g. *Au Clair de la lune*, discussed in Section 10) and to demand harmonies, directly contradicting the old notion of the characteristics of folk-song. The simplest conclusion

to draw is that the whole folk/traditional area is difficult to sum up stylistically – there is simply too much variety – but as a crude generalization, it is safe to say that (a) the more urban the origin of the tune, and (b) the later it was produced, the more likely it is to contain harmonic implications, to be influenced by instrumental phraseology, and to exist in written (and therefore relatively fixed) form.

11.4 SOME PRACTICAL WORK (III)

Here are three further melodies for you to read and play. With each one you should:

1 copy it out in both treble and bass clefs,

2 listen to each as it is played (in the appropriate clef) on the audio-cassette,

3 attempt to play it yourself on your keyboard.

Try it with separate hands first then, if you are feeling confident, with both hands together. I have given a few hints on fingering. The fingering for the last two notes in this next example may surprise you, but remember that you did try a few exercises for passing the thumb under the fingers in Video Section 2 of Unit 3.

The first tune is given as Examples 15 and 16. On the audio-cassette you will hear it sung, then played in the treble clef, then in the bass clef.

 LISTEN NOW TO ITEMS 13, 13(a) AND 13(b).

 PLAY EXAMPLES 15 AND 16.

Example 15   The Girl Who Liked Dancing

---

[4] It was Herder who invented the term *Volkslied* (folksong), and *volkstümlich* (folk-like) is a useful word to remember when discussing such melodies by Brahms and others.

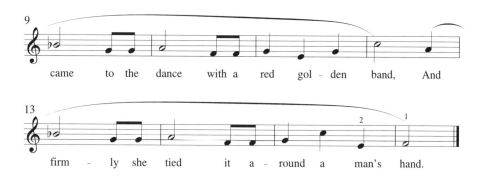

came to the dance with a red gol - den band, And

firm – ly she tied it a - round a man's hand.

Example 16   The Girl Who Liked Dancing

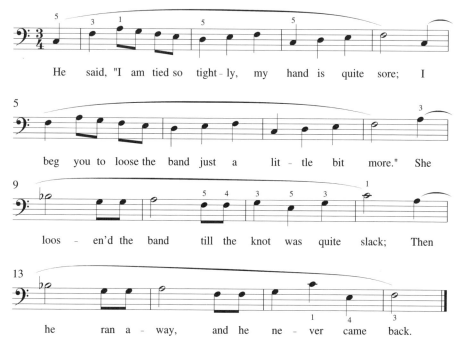

He said, "I am tied so tight - ly, my hand is quite sore; I

beg you to loose the band just a lit - tle bit more." She

loos - en'd the band till the knot was quite slack; Then

he ran a - way, and he ne - ver came back.

Incidentally, you may have thought that in Example 15 (and 16), the final bar should have had a crotchet rest after the minim to give it the correct number of beats for a ¾ bar. However, there is a notational convention that, when a tune begins with an anacrusis, as here, the rhythmic value of the

final bar is completed by the note (or notes) in the anacrusis at the start of the tune. You will see the same convention observed in the next tune.

Example 17/18 is a good example of a tune written 'in folk style' despite its apparently 'traditional' elements. The occasional individual slurs indicate that the two notes are sung to one syllable.

Again you will hear the tune sung, then played in the treble clef, and then in the bass clef.

LISTEN NOW TO ITEMS 14, 14(a) AND 14(b).

PLAY EXAMPLES 17 AND 18.

Example 17   Kelvin Grove

Let us haste to Kel - vin Grove, bon - nie las - sie O, Through its

maz - es let us rove, ___ bon - nie las - sie O, Where the

ro - ses in their pride Deck the bon - nie din - gle side, Where the

mid - night fai - ries glide, ___ bon - nie las - sie O.

Example 18   Kelvin Grove

Let us wan-der by the mill, ___ bon-nie las - sie O, To the

cove be-side the rill, ___ bon-nie las - sie O, Where the

glens re-bound the call Of the roar-ing wa-ter's fall, Through the

moun-tain's ro-cky hall, ___ bon-nie las - sie O.

Verse 3

O Kelvin banks are fair, bonnie lassie O,
When the summer we are there, bonnie lassie O,
There the may-pink's crimson plume Throws a soft but sweet
perfume
Round the yellow banks o'broom, bonnie lassie O.

The last tune in this section is *O, du lieber Augustin* (O, My Little Augustin).

Once again, the tune is sung, then played in the treble clef, then played in the bass clef on the audio-cassette.

 LISTEN NOW TO ITEMS 15, 15(a) AND 15(b).
PLAY EXAMPLES 19 AND 20.

Example 19   O, du lieber Augustin (O, My Little Augustin)

O my lit-tle Au-gus-tin, Au-gus-tin, Au-gus-tin,

O my lit-tle Au-gus-tin, ev-'ry-thing's gone! Our

mon-ey and goods are gone, All we de-pend up-on,

O my lit-tle Au-gus-tin, ev-'ry-thing's gone!

Example 20   O, du lieber Augustin

O my lit-tle Au-gus-tin, Au-gus-tin, Au-gus-tin,

O my lit-tle Au-gus-tin, ev-'ry-thing's gone! Our

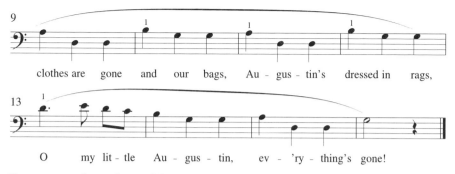

clothes are gone and our bags, Au - gus - tin's dressed in rags,

O my lit - tle Au - gus - tin, ev - 'ry - thing's gone!

You may perhaps have felt that Example 19/20 is very waltz-like. Though impossible to date, this song was almost certainly written in the early nineteenth century when the waltz began to be fashionable in Vienna and quickly spread all over Europe (but not as quickly as popular music is spread today via modern technology).

Exercise 7

(a) Name the bracketed intervals near the beginning of Examples 15, 17 and 19.

(b) Using the letters A, B, C, etc. (and ' for any developments of the appropriate letters), attempt a phrase analysis of each song.

Answers are at the end of the unit.

Discussion

You may have found *O, du lieber Augustin* difficult, and if you offered a different answer from the one given, you may well be correct. This charming tune has a built-in logic, characteristic of some German and Austrian music. You may just have noticed that the middle section (B: bars 9–12) starts by taking the last two bars of A¹ but in reverse order: bar 9 repeats bar 7, and bar 10 repeats bar 6; then bars 9–10 are repeated as bars 11–12. It can therefore be argued that only one **theme** is employed,[5] with a middle section developing a small part of the main tune (bars 1–8). This tune is therefore **monothematic**, and its middle section is developed from the first. If

this were on a larger scale, one could then describe such development as **motivic development**, since one or two **motifs**[6] (bars 3 and 4) would be treated as a new tune even though, in fact, they are not new. In this tune, the motives are not developed, but merely repeated, and therefore the term 'development' scarcely applies. You will be meeting this term later, however, since development is a particular characteristic of the music of Beethoven (and others). Put very simplistically, such composers frequently extended their music by this technique and thereby built up large musical structures.

11.5 CONCLUSIONS

Western music – that is, most music of both Western and Eastern Europe, as well as much music of both North and South America – can be said to have a distinct and in some ways separate tradition of folk music (allowing for the caution in Section 11.3) and art music. To some extent – though how far is uncertain – the two strands developed separately but they frequently interacted. We can attempt to ascribe certain characteristics to varying types of melody. There are the unsophisticated, almost static, qualities of *Suo-Gân*, the lilting, infectious gaiety of *O, My Little Augustin*, the timelessness and other-worldly atmosphere of plainsong, the simplicity of *Au Clair de la lune*, the dance-like elements of *Rosie's Skirt*, and so on. Such descriptions are, in fact, a poor substitute for the music itself; mere words are inadequate for the essential qualities of these different melodies. However, such words are a starting point for musical analysis. Of course, one already knows what these tunes are 'supposed' to convey from the song texts, but this does not lessen the difficulties of describing the tunes in words.

The difficulties of describing music increase when one moves outside one's own culture. Not only are the characteristics of music likely to be different, but the way music is created and used is likely to be different also; hence the difficulty of finding a global definition of folk-song. (The study of music of other cultures is known as **ethnomusicology**. Another definition is 'the study of music in culture'.) So, for instance, in the vast continent of Asia the intricacies of Indian music can be contrasted with the simplicities and static qualities of much Chinese and Japanese music. And much African music,

---

[5] A theme is a recognizable and recurrent series of notes. It may or may not sound complete in itself, since it frequently forms part of a larger structure. Sometimes it is similar to a tune, or melody, though the latter *is* complete in itself and does not necessarily form part of a larger piece. This will be taken up again in Unit 16.

[6] Another term I should define. A motif (also *motive* or *motto*) is a brief though recognizable group of notes, which is too short-lived and incomplete to be a theme, and is frequently used as a building-brick with which to construct a piece. A *theme* might well consist of several *motives*. Again, this concept will be discussed further in Unit 16.

excepting that of the Moslem-influenced music of North Africa, is predominantly rhythmic in nature, and of a complexity which is more than comparable with the complexities of an Indian *raga*.

I have concentrated on folk and traditional songs because some at least are reasonably familiar; those that are not are constructed in a simple and fairly obvious way. Many are therefore relatively easy to follow and play. Later units will concentrate on larger (and longer) pieces of music, but at this stage there is one exercise you should try to do as frequently as you can. Practise looking at the examples in this unit, trying to hear the tunes in your mind. This is an important aspect of aural training and an essential requirement for a musician. You will find that this musical skill will be indispensable once you start to study harmony and more advanced musical analysis. It is also useful when you look at an unfamiliar piece of music and need to offer a reasoned and balanced judgement upon it. Do start to practise this kind of non-keyboard aural training immediately, if possible using your instrument to check your efforts.

12 EIGHT FURTHER MELODIES

12.1 BEETHOVEN AND HANDEL

This section, you will be glad to hear, is brief, and is intended solely to give you some additional practice in hearing and playing some well-known melodies. Most of them are by famous composers. Sometimes I have provided versions in different keys, and I have added some slurs for your convenience. But otherwise the tunes have not been altered in any way. Play each one as often as you need to and, if you have time, copy them out. All are on your audio-cassette as Items 16–23. Note that the first two examples are notated in the bass clef and should be played with your left hand.

Example 21 is Item 16 on the audio-cassette.

  LISTEN NOW TO ITEM 16.
PLAY EXAMPLE 21.

Example 21   Beethoven, Ninth Symphony, Finale (transposed)

Example 22 gives the tune of Example 21 in its original key. The tune starts on the third degree of the scale, F♯. You can hear it played as Item 16(a).

  LISTEN NOW TO ITEM 16(a).
PLAY EXAMPLE 22.

Example 22   Beethoven, Ninth Symphony, Finale (original key)

Example 23 is at Beethoven's original pitch. Count the rests carefully and watch out for the difference between E♭ and E♮! It is Item 17 on the audio-cassette.

 LISTEN NOW TO ITEM 17.

 PLAY EXAMPLE 23.

Example 23   Beethoven, 'Waldstein' Sonata for piano, Finale

Example 24 comes from some music intended to be played out-of-doors to accompany a fireworks display. It is played as Item 18 on the audio-cassette.

 LISTEN NOW TO ITEM 18.

 PLAY EXAMPLE 24.

Example 24   Minuet from the Royal Fireworks Music *by Handel*

12.2 HAYDN

Example 25 is a minuet from a piano sonata by Haydn. In its first appearance on the audio-cassette it is transposed down one tone so that G, rather than A, is the tonic note. On the audio-cassette, this is Item 19.

 LISTEN NOW TO ITEM 19.

 PLAY EXAMPLE 25.

Example 25   Minuet by Haydn

Example 26   Minuet by Haydn

Example 26 puts this tune back into Haydn's original key. There are quite a lot of black notes here, so playing it may be a little tricky, but persevere. You may find it helpful to write the names of the notes above the stave first. In this 'real' version you can see the sign ‖: at the end of bar 10 and :‖ at the start of bar 11. These indicate that each half (bars 1–10 and 11–20) is played twice. On the audio-cassette, Items 19(a) and 19(b) observe this convention. Note that a section of music using these 'repeat signs' will have :‖ at the beginning and ‖: at the end, as in bars 11 and 20. However, bar 1 of a piece may or may not have the :‖ sign – frequently it does not, as in Example 26; however bars 1–10 will still be repeated, as here. If bars 10 and 11 had been on the same line, rather than on separate lines, then the ‖: and :‖ signs would have been back-to-back. Instead of literally putting these signs together, we use this symbol :‖: between repeated sections.

Item 19(a) consists of Example 26. Item 19(b) is as Haydn wrote this minuet, that is, it is Example 26 with the accompaniment added, the music of which I have not supplied here.

 LISTEN NOW TO ITEMS 19(a) AND 19(b).

 PLAY EXAMPLE 26.

Exercise

The structure of this melody is unusually interesting. Look at it, listen or play it again, and see if you can describe what is happening.

Answer and discussion

The structure is a tricky one to analyse. The tune moves to the half-way point at bar 10; from bar 11 the music plays backwards until it reaches the first note again. This minuet *al rovescio* (i.e. backwards), as Haydn called it, is reminiscent of the puzzle and riddle canons of the Mediaeval period, where this type of intellectual writing was relatively common. By Haydn's time (1732–1809) it was an unusual device. (It is considerably harder to do than you might think, by the way.) In his original manuscript Haydn wrote out only the first half (i.e. bars 1–10). His intellectual mastery had produced a 'first half' which, played backwards, provided a second half. This made it unnecessary to write out the second half since the music, in a sense, had already been composed. Remember, though, that, despite all this intellectual activity, each half is played twice.

12.3 CANONIC TUNES

The next two examples work in canon (see the end of Section 2.3). Note that I have not supplied the words for these examples. At this stage it would be hard to find two more contrasting examples: the first, an austere and simple tune by the great English Renaissance composer Thomas Tallis (c.1505–85), the second a traditional popular tune that everyone knows. Listen several times to Example 27 (Item 20) on your audio-cassette, even if the melody is well-known to you.

 LISTEN NOW TO ITEM 20.

Now look at Example 27. I have placed an asterisk at the point where a second part can join in, though there are several points where you can do this. For instance, in Items 20(b) and (c) on the audio-cassette you will hear the second part joining in a bar later. Find a friend to sing or play with you. You could try experimenting to see whether additional points in the music will yield a third or fourth part. The slightly unusual $\frac{4}{2}$ metre indicates that the basic beat is a minim, rather than the more usual crotchet: four minims rather than four crotchets to the bar, in other words. Items 20(a), (b) and (c) on the audio-cassette offer canonic choral versions in 2, 3 and 4 parts of this tune by Tallis.

 LISTEN NOW TO ITEMS 20(a), (b) AND (c).

Example 27   Tallis's Canon

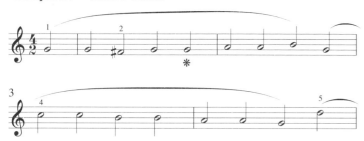

As with *Pop! Goes the Weasel*, which you studied earlier, the following nursery rhyme is in $\frac{6}{8}$. Thus, each dotted crotchet is worth three quavers. Listen to Item 21 on your audio-cassette to remind yourself of how it should go. You will hear it played on the piano, sung by the sopranos in a choir, then in two parts (women and men).

 LISTEN NOW TO ITEMS 21, 21(a) and 21(b).

Example 28   Three Blind Mice

12.4 TCHAIKOVSKY

The last two melodies in this unit come from the *Serenade for Strings*, Op. 48, by Tchaikovsky. They both appear in the last movement, and are derived from, and in fact probably are, Russian folk-songs. If you look at your score, you will see that Tchaikovsky describes this movement as 'Finale' (*Tema Russo*)[7]. As always, the short examples here are played on the audio-cassette. In each case, try to play the example first.

 PLAY EXAMPLE 29.

 LISTEN TO ITEM 22.

Example 29 Tchaikovsky, Serenade for Strings, *Finale*

By this stage, I hope that the above example posed few problems for you, since there were no black notes to play. Example 30 may be a decorated version by Tchaikovsky of a simpler form of the tune, since the semiquavers seem more suited to instrumental music than to vocal melody. As a result, you will probably find this tune very difficult to play up to speed, but it works well at a slower tempo. Items 23, 23(a) and 23(b) offer Example 30 below at three different speeds. See which suits you best.

---

[7] 'Finale' is a title sometimes used by composers for the last movement of a work, though occasionally the term can refer to a 'final' organ voluntary. *Tema Russo* means 'Russian Theme'.

Example 30 Tchaikovsky, Serenade for Strings, *Finale*

 PLAY EXAMPLE 30.

 LISTEN TO ITEMS 23, 23(a) and 23(b).

Now play the whole movement on Audio-cassette 15 to hear what Tchaikovsky does with this boisterous melody.

 LISTEN TO THE MOVEMENT ON AUDIO-CASSETTE 15.

Did you notice that Example 30 is nearly always present, almost obsessively so? This element of obsessive repetition is particularly characteristic of Russian music.

13 CONCLUSIONS AND CHECKLIST

The foregoing examples have demonstrated numerous types of melody. Their range, both melodic and emotional, is varied. Some are by composers we can name, others not. My last observation has to be a personal and subjective one. *Suo-Gân* is limited to three notes. The great melody from the finale of Beethoven's Ninth Symphony is noble and uplifting, despite a limited melodic range that is almost as restricted as that of *Suo-Gân*. Should one compare 'art' music with 'folk' music? They are essentially different, though it is difficult to explain why these differences exist. It is easy to believe that music 'of the people' must be the quintessence of great music. Some Romantics (particularly the Nationalists) must have seen it that way. The real truth is simple: folk and art are too different in themselves to be compared with each other. Many folk tunes are far finer than some melodies written by 'great' composers. In one sense, it is pointless to make comparisons. Art music is not necessarily 'better' than folk music, though for me it is certainly more satisfying. Each must be heard and assessed on its own merits.

13.1 CHECKLIST

The topics listed below are those with which you should be familiar before you proceed to Unit 5. They occur in the order in which you have studied them. You can assume that topics not listed here are for reference or for general interest, though they may be returned to or elaborated on later in the course. This applies especially to important subjects such as music history, major composers, analysis and important musical genres.

You should therefore aim to be familiar with:

1 definitions of melody,

2 its relationship to other aspects of music,

3 definitions of *canon* and *polyphony,*

4 plainsong (plainchant) (incidentally, this is sometimes known as *Gregorian* chant),

5 all the given melodies[8],

6 intervals and how to calculate them,

7 phrase and sentence,

8 phrase structures,

9 antecedent and consequent,

10 some of the contradictory definitions of folk-song,

11 a basic understanding of the interaction between 'folk' and 'art',

12 the stylistic interpenetration between 'folk' and 'traditional'.

The last three aims are, perhaps, relatively nebulous for you at this stage, and are less important than the more practical skills and historical concepts that form the bulk of the list above.

Finally, the best way to improve your keyboard and notation skills is to work at them 'little and often', rather than doggedly for a couple of hours a month.

---

[8] This is perhaps the most important item in the list, and it means that you should be able to play the simpler melodies at your keyboard and if possible 'hear' all of them mentally. You do not, of course, need to know these melodies 'by heart'.

14 ANSWERS TO EXERCISES

Exercise 1

Example 31 Suo-Gân

Exercise 2

Example 32 is *Suo-Gân* starting on the note D.

Example 32 Suo-Gân

Example 33 is *Rosie's Skirt* starting on the note D.

Example 33 Rosie's Skirt

Example 34 is *Rosie's Skirt* starting on D in the bass clef.

Example 34 Rosie's Skirt

Exercise 3

(a) Third   (d) Fourth

(b) Seventh   (e) Octave

(c) Second   (f) Unison

Exercise 4

(a) The intervals are as follows:

interval a is a second;   interval c is a third;

interval b is a third;   interval d is a second.

(b) The first and fourth lines are identical.

Exercise 5

Rosie's Skirt has the structure AABBA.

Exercise 6

Au Clair de la lune has the structure AABA, which you could well reduce to ABA.

Exercise 7

(a) The intervals are as follows:

Example 15: a fourth.

Example 17: a second.

Example 19: a third.

(b) The phrase structures are as follows:

Example 15: AABB'.

Example 17: AA'BA'.

Example 19: AA'BA'.

15 REFERENCES

Apel, W., *Harvard Dictionary of Music*, Heinemann, London, 1944.

Blom, E., 'Plainchant/plainsong' in *Everyman's Dictionary Of Music* (6th ed, revised by David Cummings), Dent, London, 1988.

Powers, H. S., 'Melody' in *New Harvard Dictionary of Music* Harvard University Press, Cambridge, Massachusetts, 1986.

Ringer, A. L., 'Melody' in *The New Grove Dictionary of Music and Musicians*, Macmillan, London, 1980.

Wachsmann, K. P., 'Folk music' in *The New Grove Dictionary of Music and Musicians*, Macmillan, London, 1980.

ACKNOWLEDGEMENT

Figure 1 Reproduced by permission of the British Library Board.

UNIT 5

HARMONY I: THE CHORD

Prepared for the Course Team by Donald Burrows

CONTENTS

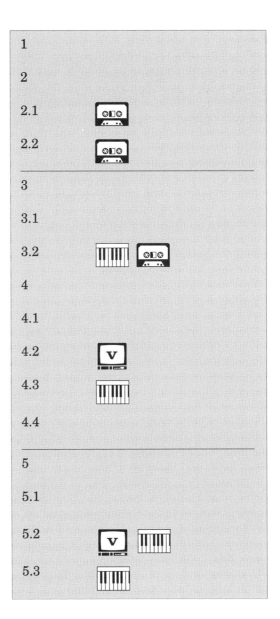

33

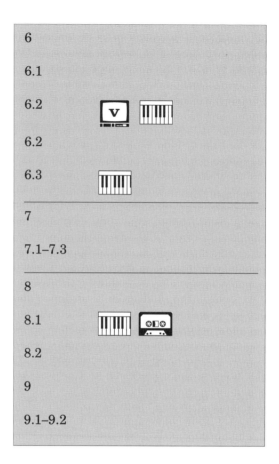

All audio items for this unit are on Audio-cassette 3.

All video items for this unit are on Video-cassette 1.

1 CONTENT AND AIMS

In the first units of the course you studied the topics of rhythm and pitch, and the way that these elements are combined into melodies. With this unit you branch out in a new direction, to study sounds in combination, as chords. After a short consideration of the relationship between melody and harmony, the unit is mainly concerned with the construction of individual chords. The principal aim of the unit is to introduce you to the 'common chord', which is basically quite a simple musical construction but can exist in a number of alternative forms or 'inversions'. You will experience the chord in three ways – heard, played (on your keyboard) and written. You will also be introduced briefly to the procedures for fitting chords under the notes of melodies.

Although the unit contains some theoretical material – on the acoustic basis for the common chord, for example – it is mainly practical, requiring you to try things out on the keyboard and on paper, and above all to listen carefully to the examples and to your own attempted solutions. The examples run throughout the unit, and from Section 3 onwards you will need keyboard, pencil and music manuscript paper by you pretty well all the time. Parts of Sections 4, 5 and 6 are on video. In Sections 5 and 6 the video sections are to be used in conjunction with the other resources: you will need your keyboard and writing materials alongside the video. It is especially important that you take the video sections at the points indicated in the unit, as they include demonstrations of techniques that are essential later.

This unit necessarily introduces a new level of technical difficulty, in that you will eventually have to use two staves together, with treble and bass clefs, in order to accommodate the high notes and low notes that sound together in most chords: hitherto, your melodies have either been in one clef or the other. But, once you have mastered the basic trick of combining the two clefs, you should have the compensating satisfaction of being able to write and play your own chords and of understanding how they are constructed.

2 THE IMPORTANCE OF HARMONY

2.1 SCHUBERT'S THEME

Listen to the opening of the fourth movement from Schubert's Octet. The extract is first played complete, then the melody and accompaniment are given separately. You will probably remember the music, which you heard in the Course Introduction.

 LISTEN NOW TO ITEMS 1(a), 1(b) AND 1(c).

From your work on melody in Unit 4, you will have realized by now that most music is not pure rhythm, or pure pitch, or pure dynamics[1], but a result of the interaction of these (and other) elements. It is relatively easy to see how rhythm, pitch and dynamics are combined in a melody, although not so easy to analyse why these complex interactions produce a really outstanding melody. But the interrelationship between melody and harmony may not have occurred to you before. Because the texture of Schubert's theme is tune-and-accompaniment, with a fairly clear separation between the melody and the accompanying harmony, you may have assumed that the composer wrote the tune first, and then thought up some chords ('the harmony') to go underneath it. This assumption may also be reinforced by many of the harmony exercises that you will encounter in this course, which are couched in terms of putting appropriate chords under a given melody.

However, melodies and accompaniments cannot be so easily separated. Some melodies, it is true, were created as self-standing entities, without need of an accompaniment – this is the case, for example, with many plainsong and folk-song melodies. (You met melodies of both types in Unit 4.) But the development of a large part of Western musical culture during the period between 1600 and 1900 was strongly influenced by harmonic considerations, and very exciting this path proved. Although harmony may often function as an accompaniment or background, our experience of Western music leads us to expectations about the way that harmony will behave[2] : and melodies, including rhythms and pitches, are frequently driven by the harmony. This may seem an extravagant statement, and indeed I admit to putting the issue in its most basic form. But I hope that the following exercise will give you some idea of the controlling force of the harmony in Schubert's theme. In order to clarify the harmony I have simplified Schubert's 'um-cha' accompaniment by combining the notes into plain chords.

Exercise 1

On the cassette the accompaniment to the first four bars is given in simple chords (Item 2a). Then the nine chords of the first phrase are repeated, with spoken identifying numbers (Item 2b). Play both extracts a couple of times, then concentrate on Item 2(b). What do you notice about (a) chords 3 and 4, and (b) chords 7 to 9?

 LISTEN NOW TO ITEMS 2(a) AND 2(b).

Discussion

The interest of the harmony lies not only in the different chords, but in the way that they move at varying speeds. The harmony 'waits' at chords 3 and 4, and 'hurries' at chords 7 to 9. If I represented the duration of the chords by horizontal lines in equivalent lengths, a simple diagram of the chord changes would be as shown in Figure 1.

beats	1	2	3	4	5	6	7	8
chord movement	——	——	————		——	——	—	—
chords	1	2	3	4	5	6	7	8	9

Figure 1

You'll notice that I've shown chords 3 and 4 as a single long line – although two chords are played, the second repeats the harmony of the first, so there is no *change* in the harmony.

---

[1] 'Dynamics' is the word normally used by practical musicians to refer to the 'volume' element in a sound, whether in a smooth gradation from *piano* (soft) to *forte* (loud) or in a more sudden change of volume to produce a momentary stress or accent.

[2] This experience is now almost instinctive, being based on a long-established historical awareness of what we perceive as 'correct'.

Listen to Items 2(a) and 2(b) again, following the diagram, to check what I have said about the chord movement.

 LISTEN AGAIN TO ITEMS 2(a) AND 2(b).

2.2 HARMONIC RHYTHM

From Exercise 1, I hope you can appreciate that the accompaniment has a layer of interest of its own, independent of the melody. The harmony in itself has a rhythm, moving slowly in some places, faster in others: this is called **harmonic rhythm**. This rhythm gives a sense of onward movement to the music: in other words, the chords do not just exist as single entities, but are arranged in relation to each other. The chords give a sense of **progression**, of moving forward in some places, and of resting at 'goal' points such as the end of a phrase. Although the practical part of this unit is concerned with individual chords, these chords will eventually go into contexts of surrounding chords that give them their 'meaning'. That is, they will become part of chord progressions. You may only need two successive chords to give this sense of chord progression, though the similar phrase 'harmonic progression' usually implies the organization of harmony on a longer span.

Now listen to Item 2(a) twice more, imagining how the tune fits on top. You might try singing the tune over the accompaniment.

 LISTEN AGAIN TO ITEM 2(a).

Then replay Item 1(a) to restore Schubert's original. Try to listen for the chord structure without being distracted by the scoring of the 'um-cha' accompaniment. (The simple chords, with the melody, are given as Example 1. You may find it helpful to follow this at the last play-through.)

 LISTEN AGAIN TO ITEM 1(a).

By now I hope you realize that the harmony of Schubert's theme is virtually inseparable from the melody. The melody was written not only according to its own parameters of rhythm and pitch, but also with reference to an underlying harmonic rhythm and a sense of chord movement – the chord (or harmonic) progression of the complete phrase. Schubert's harmonic scheme

Example 1

Melody

Accompaniment

shaped the melody, and he must have developed the two together when composing the theme.

Schubert's theme is a particularly elegant example of the interaction between melody and harmony. Although it doesn't use any chords that are unusual in themselves, they are arranged in a particularly pleasing rhythm and progression. But the shaping of melodies through the sense of direction imposed by harmonic rhythm is not only a feature of music by composers such as Schubert that we now regard as part of 'high art'. 'Harmonic' thinking has also dominated other areas of western music-making. For another example, we can go to *The Mistletoe Bough* (c.1835), a nineteenth-century ballad with music by Henry Bishop (1786-1855). Listen to Item 3, which is verse 1 of the ballad.

 LISTEN NOW TO ITEM 3.

Obviously the texture of the ballad is tune (i.e. melody, sung by the voice) and accompaniment (piano), which might lead you to regard the music as being simply divided between melody (voice) and accompanying harmony (piano). Yet this piece presents an even clearer example than Schubert's of a melody composed 'on the back' of the harmony. As a melody, the tune is relatively uninspired: it relies on the 'drive' of the harmony (the accompaniment). If you were composing an unaccompanied melody, you probably would not choose to set the first eleven syllables of the text to the same note.[3]

---

[3] Some genuinely unaccompanied ballad melodies do, of course, include repeated notes: the point about this particular example is that the harmony of the first chord is held for a long time, carrying several syllables of the text.

The shape of the melody after the first eleven notes seems to me to be controlled by the harmonic rhythm and the background of a fairly conventional series of chord progressions. (It is the very conventional nature of this chord-background at the beginning that gives force to the slightly more adventurous turn of the harmony in the last phrases of the verse.) Even if you took the accompaniment away, it would not be too difficult to 'hear' (i.e. imagine) the chords implied by the melody, because of the simplicity and strength of the harmonic background.

Now listen to the song again, concentrating on the harmony: remember that both the voice and the piano (with its 'um-cha-cha' accompaniment) decorate a quite simple succession of chords. Try to hear the chords as entities, irrespective of the foreground of melodic and rhythmic decoration: listen for when the chords *change*, thereby gaining a sense of the chord progressions.

 LISTEN AGAIN TO ITEM 3.

Exercise 2

Here is the melody (Example 2), marked with arrows to show where the rhythmical beats come. The harmony does not change every beat. Sometimes the same chord will be repeated for two beats, or even for two bars. Listen to the song again and then, below the words, try to represent the chord movement (i.e. the length of time that a particular chord lasts before it changes to the next one) with horizontal lines similar to those I used for the Schubert theme in Figure 1. The 'answer' is given at the end of the unit.

Example 2

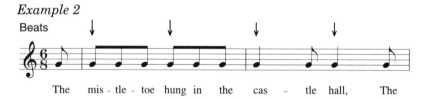

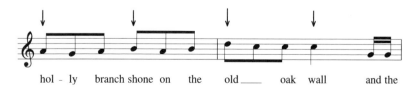

Oh! the mis - tle - toe bough,

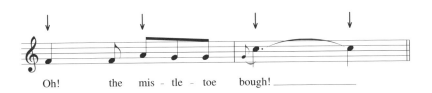

Oh! the mis - tle - toe bough!

When you compare my answer to Exercise 2 with your version, you may find quite a few differences, and there could be several reasons for this: the melody has a few decorations that may have distracted you from the harmony, for example, and you are less familiar with this music than with Schubert's theme. At the moment, it's less important that you get all the details right than that you begin to develop the skill of listening to the harmony without being too distracted by the melody.

Now listen to the song (Item 3) once more, following the 'answer' diagram, and try to keep your attention wholly on the harmony.

 LISTEN AGAIN TO ITEM 3.

3 THE SINGLE CHORD

3.1 INTRODUCTION

It is important that you try to develop your aural skills in order to hear chord changes and chord progressions, but you obviously will not be able to *write* complete chord progressions at first, and still less are you likely to be able to play them fluently on the keyboard immediately. These are skills that will

be built up as you work through the following units. We must begin by considering the single unit of the chord, as the first step in the process.

3.2 CONCORDS AND DISCORDS

> A chord is produced when different pitches are sounded simultaneously.

You can regard any combination of simultaneously sounding notes of different pitches as a chord. In describing particular chords as 'discords' or 'concords'[4] we make a partly subjective, and cultural, evaluation based on our received ideas of dissonance and consonance. As a rough guide, a consonance is a chord that seems to be complete in itself, so that (for example) it could satisfactorily come at the end of a piece of music. The following section of the unit builds on your work from Unit 4, in particular Video Section 1 of that unit and its accompanying exercise.

You may perhaps be wondering whether there is a maximum or minimum number of simultaneous notes that can constitute a chord. Strictly the answer is 'no', although we more often refer to a two-note chord as an interval. This may be a little confusing because you have already met intervals as measures of melodic pitch-distance. A harmonic interval is merely two notes of different pitches sounded at the same time. As with other types of chords, we perceive intervals in terms of consonance and dissonance.

Exercise 3

 Find the two notes of Example 3 on your keyboard: play them one after another and then play them simultaneously. When sounded simultaneously (as a 'harmonic interval') they are ranged vertically, as in Example 4.

Example 3

---

[4] Notice, incidentally, the spellings of 'discord' and 'concord', which lose the 'h' from 'chord'.

Example 4

Play them again. Do you hear this interval as a consonance (concord) in which the notes blend well together, or as a dissonance (discord)? I give my answer at the end of the unit.

Exercise 4

Now do the same for Example 5, (a) to (f). Find the notes, play each pair together, and then write below each interval either 'C' for concord or 'D' for discord.

Example 5

(a)　(b)　(c)　(d)　(e)　(f)

These intervals are played as audio-cassette Item 4. After you have tried playing them for yourself, listen to Item 4 as a check that you have found the right notes, and as a final cross-check on your answers.

 CHECK WITH ITEM 4.

Discussion

There's obviously a subjective element here, and it would be wrong to speak of 'right' answers in absolute terms. I expect that you agreed with at least most of my answers. But even if you did, you have to remember that you are hearing the intervals out of musical and historical context. The interval at Example 5(b) sounds consonant to us, but in the Middle Ages it was a subject of theoretical controversy, and opinions differed as to whether that sound (the interval of a third) should be accepted as a consonance. In terms of earlier styles, it was a dissonant sound. And, although the notes of Example 5(f) blend well together, this interval (a 'perfect' fourth) behaves as a dissonance in many musical contexts. You might regard

the first case, the interval of a third, as an example of a simple historical change of taste in the matter of chords; but the second case opens up a special and more complex issue of harmonic context to which I shall return in Section 8 of this unit.

In isolating single chords or intervals, we are necessarily creating an artificial situation. The development of the Western harmonic system has been constantly stimulated by the interaction between 'harmony' (the simultaneous sounding of notes) and 'counterpoint' (the simultaneous presentation of two or more independent tunes, which you know from Unit 4 is described as polyphony). Example 6, for example, consists of two simultaneous strands of melody, one in each clef:[5]

Example 6　J. S. Bach, Two-part Invention in D minor, BWV 775

In terms of the conventions of our musical notation, I would describe the separate strands of melody in Example 6 as the 'horizontal' element. But of course from bar 3 onwards two tunes are sounding at the same time, so there is a 'vertical' element as well. The notes sounded simultaneously form two-note chords (or intervals). Two of these chords are indicated by boxes in Example 7.

---

[5]　The signs at the end of the music are called 'directs': they show the pitches of the next notes at the end of the extract.

Example 7   J. S. Bach, Two-part Invention in D minor, BWV 775

The chords from the boxes are given separately as Example 8.

Example 8

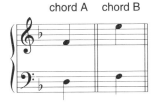

Exercise 5

The two chords from Example 8 are played on the audio-cassette as Item 5. Listen to them and assess them as concords or discords.

 LISTEN NOW TO ITEM 5.

I expect that you did not have too much disagreement with my answers. But now listen to the chords in context. Example 6 is recorded as audio-cassette Item 6. Listen to it a few times now. After a couple of hearings, try following the music from Example 7 while you listen to it again. You should be able to follow the general shape of the melodic lines from the sound.

 LISTEN NOW TO ITEM 6.

When you heard the complete extract, it's very doubtful that you would have been aware of the dissonance at chord 'B'. Your attention was distracted from the dissonance by the logic of the 'horizontal' element – that is, by the way the tunes fit together. And, in context, this dissonance was only a detail. Most of the harmonies were concords, and there was a strong harmonic rhythm of chord progressions in the background. So our perception of whether a particular interval or chord is a consonance or a dissonance is affected by the counterpoint (that is, by the way the tunes move and combine 'horizontally'), and by our perception of the harmonic rhythm. The same chord or interval may behave as a consonance in one context and as a dissonance in another.

4   THE COMMON CHORD AND ITS ACOUSTIC FOUNDATIONS

4.1   INTRODUCTION

Notwithstanding the last point, there is a norm for the basic consonant chord in the main repertory of Western music. And, although our perception of this type of chord is determined partly by subjective or cultural assumptions, it is also true that the chord has a basis in physical and acoustic phenomena. The first part of this section, on video-cassette, is included to give you an understanding of the acoustic background. You do not have to memorize this material, but please follow it carefully as it should help you to understand the basic pattern of the common chord.

4.2   HARMONICS AND THE HARMONIC SERIES

 **VIDEO NOTES
UNIT 5, VIDEO SECTION 1**

Introduction

There are no notes to read during this video section. The notes below are for reference and revision.

NOW WATCH THE VIDEO SECTION.

Summary

The complete length of a string or a tube (for a wind instrument) produces a fundamental pitch. Harmonics are pitches which are produced by dividing this complete length in simple ratios. If the length is halved, the frequency of the pitch is doubled; if the length is divided by three, the frequency of the pitch is trebled, and so on. In physics, the fundamental note is called the first harmonic, the note with double the frequency is called the second harmonic, and so on.

When an instrument plays a note (or a singer sings a note) we may think that we hear a single note. But most instruments produce sounds with a mixture of harmonics of different intensities. That is, several harmonically related frequencies are sounding at once. On a stringed instrument it is possible to pick out the harmonics by touching the string lightly at the points of ratio division. On a brass instrument (such as the French horn) the way the notes are produced allows the player to pick out the individual harmonics and make each one in turn the principal sounding note.

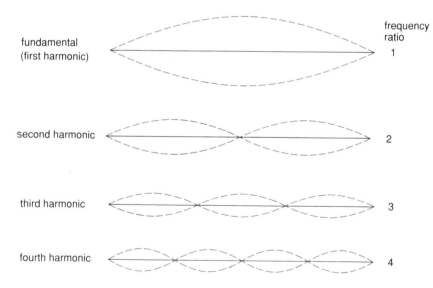

Figure 2   Fundamental frequency and harmonics, and corresponding vibration patterns.

The notes produced by the successive harmonic ratios are known as the **harmonic series**. A harmonic series on the fundamental note C would have the notes shown in Video Example 1. The numbers below the notes indicate the multiplication of the fundamental frequency.

Video Example 1

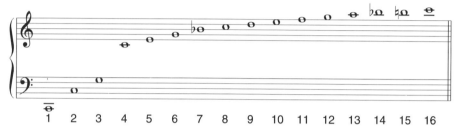

Note. From harmonic 7 onwards, some of the notes are not precisely 'in tune' with the expectations of our modern pitch system, so the notes given here are rather approximate (in particular, notes 7 and 11). Furthermore, because of the nature of individual instruments, some of the harmonics are easier or harder to produce than others, so this is a slightly artificial complete scheme of theoretically possible notes. The horn player on the videocassette produces harmonics 2–16, first on a fundamental note of F, then on C – but sounding an octave lower than shown here.

Combinations of the fundamental and the lower harmonics – those with the simplest ratios – generally produce an agreeable sound. A frequency that does not bear a simple ratio to the fundamental cannot be fitted into a tidy vibration pattern. For instance, a string cannot vibrate in such a way as to produce the harmonic shown in Figure 3.

Figure 3   A vibration pattern that would fit 2.7 times in the length of the string.

Mixing the note in Figure 3 with one of the notes of the original harmonic series would produce a dissonance.

4.3 CONSTRUCTING THE COMMON CHORD FROM THE HARMONIC SERIES

Remembering that notes whose frequencies are in a simple ratio to each other tend to sound well together, we should be able to produce an agreeable chord by putting together the first few notes of the harmonic series from Video Example 1 and sounding them at the same time, as in Example 9.

Example 9

Exercise 6

> The bottom note of this series is C (because I chose that note as the fundamental), and the notes taken together form a 'chord of C'. Work out the letter names of the other notes, and write them in the spaces here (I have put in the first one): C _ _ _ _ _ .

Try playing Example 9 on your keyboard. Find the notes separately first, before trying to play them all together. Then try assembling the chord gradually. Play the highest note with the little finger of your right hand and then – still holding this note down – add on the one below, and so on. You should just about be able to play the complete chord, by taking the top four notes with your right hand and the lowest two with your left hand. If you cannot stretch all of the notes comfortably, leave out the bottom note and spread the others as is most comfortable. Listen carefully both to the complete chord, and to the sound-combinations as you build the chord up.

 PLAY EXAMPLE 9.

When you have mastered the complete chord, try building it up gradually again, but this time beginning from the bottom note and working upwards. Again listen carefully as you add the notes on, and listen to the sound of the complete chord. Then experiment with leaving out one note of the chord (a different one each time) and listening carefully to the resulting effect.

Exercise 7

We now examine the musical properties of the chord. Use the 'feel' of the chord on the keyboard, as well as its appearance in notation, to help you to answer the following questions:

(a) How many different notes are there in the chord? (Think carefully! There are two possible answers, and both are required.)

(b) What do you notice about the number relationships (in Example 9) of the notes that have the same letter names?

(c) What do you notice about the spacing of the chord, that is, the relative distances between the notes in the chord?

The answers are given at the end of the unit.

Discussion

Those answers may have seemed rather elementary but they indicate the most important principles of chord-construction. Taking each point separately:

(a) You would not expect a chord with many notes to have an equally large number of note names. In a chord of C, like this one, you use the basic notes C, G, E as many times as is convenient at different pitch-levels. The re-use of the same note name at different pitch-levels (i.e. at different octaves) is called **doubling**. 'Common chords' are indeed built from combinations of only three different note names.

(b) Here we have accidentally encountered not only the basis for chord construction but also the acoustic basis for our system of note names. Notes whose frequencies are in a 2:1 ratio blend so well together that we almost hear them as different versions of the same note. That's why we call them by the same name. The octave (that is, the interval between two notes in a 2:1 frequency ratio, and thus with the same note name) is such a consonant interval that we sometimes have to be careful how it is used. In later units we shall consider harmony not merely as chords but also as the combination of 'parts' or tunes (the 'horizontal' aspect that I referred to at the end of Section 3). When you come to write your own harmony you must be careful that two parts do not simply double the same tune an octave apart, because they thereby lose their independence and sound like one part only.

As an optional experiment, you might like to try out the sound of a few octaves on your keyboard. Then you might like to have another go at playing the opening of *Suo-Gân* in octaves as you did in Unit 4, one hand at each octave:

Example 10   Suo-Gân *in octaves*

You'll quickly discover whether you are playing the right notes. If you are, the tunes from the two hands will almost blend into one: if not, the result will be very dissonant!

(c)   The spacing of the notes in a chord is affected by many different factors arising from the musical context. It is nevertheless true that the most pleasing individual chords have larger spacings in the lower register than in the upper register. This is an acoustically guaranteed safe principle when you are constructing chords and choosing which notes to put where. But, of course, the arrangement of individual parts or tunes might not always allow you to space the notes of a chord in this way. And also, on some occasions, you might deliberately want a more gritty or heavy sonority (that is, sound quality) for the chord, which would require a less 'natural' spacing. Nevertheless, it's a good general practice to avoid bunching notes low down in a chord; otherwise, the chord will probably have a muddy texture.

I have made out a case for 'the basic chord' – or, to give it its proper name now, the **common chord** – as a natural product of the harmonic series. But, though I did not actually cheat, I admit that I exercised some initial control over the example by choosing to stop at note 6 of the harmonic series. If you start to add notes such as 7, 9 and 11 of the harmonic series from Video Example 1, the conventional concord from Example 9 turns into a rather cluttered dissonance. (You can try playing the resulting chord if you like, but you'll need a friend to help you sound all the notes at the same time.)

There is a serious defence for the selection of notes 1–6, however, for obviously the harmonic ratios include more messy (and thus more dissonant) ones as you go further up. The ratios of 1:2, 1:3 from the bottom note are

simple ones, and bring with them the 'doubles' of 1:4 and 1:6. The ratio of 1:5 is just about simple enough to sound well together (this produces the interval of the third[6], from C to E, whose consonant status in the mediaeval world was dubious), but thereafter the ratio patterns become fairly awkward. So perhaps it's not surprising that the most pleasant consonances only 'work' up to about 1:6, and that the consonant chord is built only from those notes or their octave-multiples.

4.4   MAJOR AND MINOR CHORDS

In order to be completely conscientious, we also need to note one other fact. The 'major' common chord we have produced at Example 9 is to some extent natural in its acoustic construction. But there are also 'minor' chords, which are treated as having the same consonant status, even though they include one altered note that is not part of the first steps of the harmonic series. In a C minor chord, for example, the E in Example 9 would be replaced by an E♭. To that extent, minor chords are perhaps not so 'natural' in their origins. Major and minor scales and keys are subjects of later units, but it can briefly be said here that major and minor keys behave in similar ways. So if a major-key piece of music ends consonantly with a major chord, a piece in a minor key may similarly conclude with a minor chord, which we accept as being consonant. But even this is not strictly true. Up to the end of the seventeenth century (and often thereafter) composers usually preferred to end minor-key pieces with a bright major chord – a tribute to the naturally consonant qualities of the major common chord.

5   TRIADS

5.1   THE TRIAD

The common chord of C major that we examined in the previous section included notes with just three different pitch names. Because we approached the chord on the basis of the harmonic series, these three names were identified (working upwards in Example 9) in the order C, G, E. When

---

6   The E (frequency 5) is a third above the C immediately below (frequency 4). The E is obviously a much bigger interval from the C which is the fundamental. Strictly this would be a 17th, but you can regard this C–E interval as a straightforward expansion of the simple third. Expansions beyond the octave are called 'compound intervals'.

analysing the content of chords, however, it is more convenient to re-arrange the pitches into a simple ascending pattern, C, E, G. This gives us, as our principal building-block for chords, the **triad**, which gives all the pitch names we need, grouped together in 'close position' as shown in Example 11.

Example 11   Close-position triad (C major)

The word 'triad' is obviously related to 'three'. There are three notes, and furthermore the adjacent notes of the triad are the interval of a third away from one another. Going from lowest to highest, the three notes of a triad are described as the root, the third and the fifth, respectively. The triad is, in some respects, an abstract concept, or perhaps you might describe it as a kit from which you can construct chords. The next tasks are to find out about the nature of the triad itself, and then to find out how to use it to construct chords.

5.2   PLAYING TRIADS

 VIDEO NOTES
UNIT 5, VIDEO SECTION 2

Introduction

You will need to use your keyboard as you work through this video section. Keep the following notes open as well, for reference. You will be asked to play the Video Examples.

 NOW WATCH THE VIDEO SECTION.
YOU WILL ALSO NEED YOUR KEYBOARD.

During the video section

The first time you are asked to stop the tape, play Video Example 2 using the fingering shown in Figure 4 for the right hand.

Video Example 2   A triad of C major

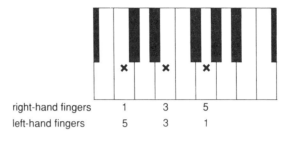

Figure 4   Playing a triad of C major. The crosses mark the notes that you play. The number 1 represents the thumb.

The second time you are asked to stop the tape, play Video Example 2 using the left-hand fingering from Figure 4. Also, play Video Example 3 (you will have to change from left-hand fingering to right-hand fingering as you move to the treble clef).

Video Example 3   Five triads of C major, low to high

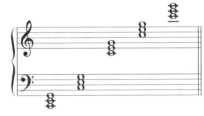

The third time you are asked to stop the tape, you should play Video Example 4.

Video Example 4   Up and down – triads on the keyboard white notes

Now try listening to some triads that you play. First play the triad on C again. You know that this a major triad. Listen carefully, not just to the pitch of the notes, but to the character of the triad as a **combination** of notes.

PLAY IT NOW.

Now (after the pause that is produced by reading these sentences) play the white-note triad on D – that is, the triad with D as its lowest note. The notes are D–F–A. Use the same hand-position as for C–E–G but one note higher. You should hear that this triad has a different character from the one on C. It sounds not merely higher, but different.

 **PLAY IT NOW.**

The triad on D is not a major triad, it is a minor triad. The difference in character is produced by the intervals within the triad.

5.3 MAJOR AND MINOR TRIADS

The best way to experience the difference between a major triad and a minor triad is to play (and listen carefully to) the different forms of the triad built on the same note.

Figure 5 is the diagram for the D minor triad.

 **PLAY IT AGAIN.**

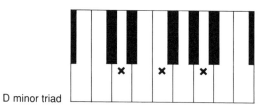

Figure 5   D minor triad

You can turn this into a major triad by altering just one note. With your middle finger play the adjacent black note (F♯) in place of the F natural. The pattern is shown on Figure 6.

 PLAY IT NOW AND LISTEN CAREFULLY.

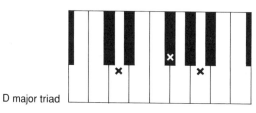

Figure 6   D major triad

Example 12 shows the D minor and D major triads in staff notation, in the treble clef (for your right hand) and in the bass clef (for your left hand).

Example 12

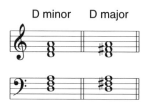

Now try playing alternately the minor triad (D–F–A) and the major triad (D–F♯–A), listening carefully for the differences in character or quality. Try minor followed by major with your right hand, and then with your left hand.

 PLAY THE TRIADS NOW.

Now repeat this exercise with the triad on C. You could turn C major into C minor by altering the middle note, playing the adjacent black note (E♭) in place of the E. Try this now, and listen carefully. The finger positions are shown in Figure 7, and the triads are given in staff notation at Example 13.

 PLAY THE TRIADS NOW.

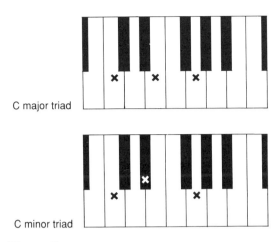

C major triad

C minor triad

Figure 7

Example 13

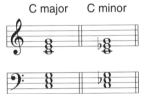

C major   C minor

You will have gathered from what you have just done that it is the third (or middle note) of the triad that makes the difference between major and minor. The minor third (e.g. C to E♭, or D to F♮) is a smaller interval than the major third (C to E, or D to F♯).

A major third (e.g. C to E) comprises four semitone steps, and a minor third (e.g. C to E♭) comprises three steps. (You might like to check that by counting them for yourself.) The major triad and the minor triad pile up their thirds in opposite ways, as Example 14 shows.

Example 14

Triad of C major   Triad of C minor

⌐ Minor 3rd   ⌐ Major 3rd
⌐ Major 3rd   ⌐ Minor 3rd

It is obviously the *lower* third that defines the triad itself as being major or minor.

You might perhaps hear the major triad as 'happy' and the minor triad as 'sad', although this is a rather subjective association and such emotional equivalence may not have been commonly recognized before the seventeenth century.

Exercise 8

Now, taking a pause between each one, try out all of the 'white note' triads (that is, those in Video Example 4). Then, in order to reduce the power of the relationships between one triad and the next, jumble the order you play them: something like F, B, E, A, C, G, D. Decide whether each one is major or minor. Listen very carefully to each one, holding it for at least five seconds, repeating it as often as you wish and then leaving a short pause before you attempt the next one. In the following grid, fill in 'M' for major triads, 'm' for minor triads and 'o' for 'others' – that is, any that seem to be of some other type. (Answers are given at the end of the unit.)

Triad	C	D	E	F	G	A	B
Type	M	m					

If you found any different answers, try playing them again, once more mixing the order so that you hear each triad individually. You might also double-check by counting the semitones between the lower two notes of any triad about which you are uncertain.

Exercise 9

Try to construct major and minor triads on any notes of the keyboard, simply 'using your ears' to attain the right sounds. Remembering the constant 1–3–5 fingering pattern, choose any note, black or white, as your root note (this will be played by the thumb of your right hand, or little finger of your left hand), and try to construct major and minor triads above, playing around with adjacent notes (using both black and white notes) and searching for the third and fifth until you produce the right sound. Make a note of your findings on the keyboard diagrams given in the answer to this question. If you try to find, for example, the major triad on the note B, put crosses on the notes that produce the right combination of sounds. Then, later in the week, you might try playing the notes from your diagram again and checking that they still sound like a major or minor triad.

6   TRIADS INTO CHORDS

6.1   CONSTRUCTING A COMMON CHORD

At the beginning of Section 5, I took the spread-out common chord generated by the first notes of the harmonic series (Example 9) and reduced (or perhaps compressed) it to its simplest analytical form – the triad (Example 11). Now we shall reverse the process, taking the notes of triads and spreading them out to form larger chords. To help you to form your own chords, there are a few basic rules, of almost universal application ('almost', because musical context can bend rules). The first is simply:

- **The notes of a common chord contain only the notes of the triad.**

This may seem so basic as to be naïve, but it covers a very common area of error. You may find this rule harder to keep than you might imagine, particularly if the skills of working out pitch names in the two clefs are new to you. When you write or play a chord, the first thing to check is that (for example) a chord of C contains only Cs, Es and Gs, **and no others**. In these early stages, when you are writing a chord it is a good practice to write the letter names of the triad next to (or under) the chord like this:

C

E

G

so that it is easy to check the rule.

Now we need to look into the question of the relationship between chords (or triads) and the melody they accompany. For the earlier part of the unit, in order to simplify the argument, I treated 'melody' and 'harmony' (the accompaniment) as two separate things. But of course that will not suffice any more. If a melody note sounds at the same time as a chord in the accompaniment, then that melody note is *part* of the harmony. We need to lay down some guidelines to make sure that everything fits together properly.

6.2   FITTING TRIADS TO MELODY NOTES

   VIDEO NOTES
UNIT 5, VIDEO SECTION 3

Introduction

You should have your keyboard, a pencil and music manuscript paper to hand as you work though this video section.

Remember the rule from Section 6.1. The notes of the common chord contain only the notes of the triad.

   NOW WATCH THE VIDEO SECTION.
YOU WILL ALSO NEED YOUR KEYBOARD.

During the video section

The first time you are asked to stop the tape, play the note F with the right hand and try other white-note triads against it with the left hand. When you have found a triad that fits, write down the name of the root note. See how many triads you can find. Video Example 6 in the summary gives you one example of a triad that fits and one that doesn't.

The second time you are asked to stop the tape, play the triads shown in Video Example 7 in the summary. Try to hear the differences between major, minor and diminished.

At the end of the video section you are asked a question which is repeated here as Exercise 10

> *Exercise 10*
>
> Which (white-note) triads fit the melody note A? The answers are at the end of the unit.

Summary

The new rule:

- **A note in a melody must be included in the triad that accompanies that note.**

In other words, the accompaniment must 'fit' or harmonize the melody note. You might find it useful to have the same rule stated from another viewpoint:

- **A melody note must be one of the notes belonging to the triad that accompanies it.**

In time you will learn practical exceptions to this rule, but it is a necessary starting-point.

Video Example 6 gives examples of triads that do, and do not, fit the melody note F.

Video Example 6

Triad on F   Triad on C

The triad on F (F, A, C) contains the note F, and thus 'fits' the melody note. The triad on E contains the notes E, G, B and does not 'fit' the melody note F.

Video Example 7 shows triads containing (and hence 'fitting') F.

Video Example 7

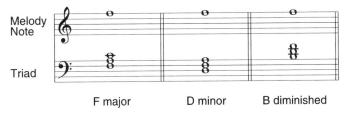

F major   D minor   B diminished

The first of these is a major triad, the second a minor triad and the third a diminished triad. You do not have to know anything about diminished triads at this stage of the course, but you will, I am sure, recognize that this triad has a characteristic sound, different from major and minor triads.

The triads in Video Example 7 'work' because they contain the melody note that they are accompanying. The melody note is F and the triads respectively have the notes:

F, A, C

D, F, A

B, D, F.

Obviously you could have calculated that (and ended up with the right answer) without recourse to the keyboard. But I hope that the experience of trying out the triads on the keyboard first has established in your mind that, if you follow the rules on paper correctly, the music will sound right. It will still take you quite a long time before you can relate harmony on paper to the sounds represented by the notation, and in the meantime you should take every opportunity to try out at the keyboard the things that you write down – and, conversely, to write down things you discover to be successful at the keyboard.

6.3 CONSTRUCTING A COMMON CHORD – CONTINUED

Taking stock of the story so far, the guidance you have received is that a common chord is constructed from the notes of the triad (and no others) and that, consequently, the melody note must be part of the chord. In terms of the exercises that you will be attempting later in the course, that last rule mainly works in reverse: you will be given the melody note and you have to find a chord that will 'fit' it.

Let us return now to the construction of chords themselves. You can produce a chord by spreading out and re-using ('doubling') the notes of the triad. A chord of C, for example, will distribute Cs, Es and Gs, spread out and doubled in various permutations. The Schubert extract with which you commenced this unit began with just such a chord.

In Item 7 of the audio-cassette you will find twenty chords of C major. They all sound different because the notes have been spread out, and distributed among various instruments, in different ways. Yet harmonically speaking they are all the same chord, a chord of C major. Listen to them now.

 LISTEN NOW TO ITEM 7.

Although any chord with Cs, Es and Gs constitutes a chord of C major, you may be asking yourself whether you are entirely free to spread the notes around in any way you like. The answer is that, while such freedom is theoretically possible, there are certain practical limitations; and there are certain aesthetic choices. Some chords (or rather chord-arrangements) sound better than others. Furthermore, the choice of chord-arrangement may be indicated by the harmonic context – that is, by the arrangement of the surrounding chords.

The practical limitations may include the following:

1 The number of voice or instrumental parts available. When writing for a four-voice choir, for example, you can use four-part (four-note) chords. If you are writing for a large orchestra, you can spread yourself into ten-part chords or more.

2 The layout of the chord may be affected by the ranges of voices or instruments: a girls' choir, for example, may not be able to use notes in the lower half of the bass clef. You will already be aware of a comparable limitation at the keyboard – the span of the human hand!

A few general rules may, however, be given about the arrangement of chords from triads:

- **It is undesirable to 'bunch' notes in the lower register.**

You have already met this principle, when you examined the spacing of the common chord derived from the harmonic series.

- **Chords should contain the root and the third. The fifth can sometimes be omitted.**

The root and the third establish the character of the chord. The interval of the third at the bottom of the triad is important because it clarifies whether the chord is major or minor. So you must include both of these notes. For the moment it is also best to try to include the fifth, because in some contexts a fifth-less chord can be ambiguous. Look, for example, at Example 15. The notes F and A, alone, might suggest *either* a chord of F major – F, A, C – *or* a chord of D minor – D, F, A. Nevertheless, in many unambiguous contexts the notes F and A, suitably spaced and doubled, can serve perfectly well as representing a chord of F major.

Example 15

F major   D minor

- **In general, it is best not to double the third of a major triad.**

The reasons for this are acoustic, and once again the effect depends on context. But it is a useful working rule. It does not apply to chords constructed from minor or diminished triads, nor to chords with six or more notes.

Exercise 11

Look at the following twelve chords (Example 16). Comment on each one, either judging it a 'good' chord that obeys all the rules given so far (with perhaps an additional comment if some feature is striking), or pointing out where the chord disobeys the rules. List your comment on each one before proceeding to the next. Assess them both by 'eye' (reading the music) and by 'ear' (playing them). In order to play some of them, you may have to divide the notes between the hands with some cunning. When in doubt, assemble the chords gradually, as you did when playing Example 9. The answers are at the end of the unit.

Example 16

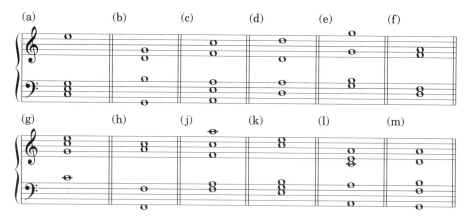

7 THE IMPORTANCE OF THE BASS: ROOTS AND INVERSIONS

7.1 A NEW COMPLICATION

I deliberately left out one of the most important rules for chords from the last section, because it is so important that it deserves a section to itself. It is this:

- **In a root position chord, the root of the triad must always be in the bass.**

That rule contains a number of words and ideas that need further explanation. The easiest is the word 'bass'. You have already encountered the word as indicating a lower register of pitches, as in 'the notes of the bass clef'. But when describing chords, the word has a more specific meaning: the bass of a chord is simply the lowest sounding part. From now on you have to distinguish between **bass**, which is the lowest sounding note or part, and **root,** which is the fundamental or generating note for the other notes of the triad, and thus for all chords derived from the triad.

Up to now, the root and the bass have been identical for all the exercises and examples in the unit. In other words the root note of the triad has also been the lowest sounding note of the triad or chord. We now have to consider what happens if we take some other note of the triad as the bass note. This requires some introductory explanation.

The previous rules have been concerned with *all* of the notes of the triad. If you have the notes C, E and G in the chord (or in some cases only C and E), it doesn't matter from the point of view of the chord itself which of these is chosen as, for example, the top note. Furthermore, you have a large choice about the way that you space the notes in the chord, the way you double them, the number of possible notes in the chord and so on. Often you will have no choice about the highest note of a chord, because it will be a melody note that has to be harmonized (although sometimes the melody can be in one of the middle-range voices), but to a large extent the arrangement of the notes in the rest of the chord below the melody note is a free-for-all.

But not absolutely. The fact is that our aural perception of a chord is critically influenced by what happens in the lowest part. The bass part is the foundation of the chord. Just as the top part is usually the critical part for the melody, so the bass part is the critical part for the harmony. The effect of a C major chord is materially changed according to whether C, E or G is in

the bass: the chord sounds significantly different. For that reason, the bass is usually the most important note in a chord.

I realize that the separation of the idea of 'root' and 'bass' provides a sudden increase in the difficulty of dealing with chords. It means leaving the safety of a situation where you knew that, for example, a chord with C in the bass would always have the notes C, E and G above. In fact, your first real exercises in harmonization in the following units will be confined for some time to 'safe' **root position** chords in which the bass note is also the root. When a note other than the root is in the bass, the chord is said to be an **inversion**. You will not need to *use* chord inversions for some time, but you need to know what they are in order to gain a full understanding of the concept of 'the chord'. By the end of this unit you should be able to cope with the analysis of inversions, and be able to write isolated examples.

The term 'inversion' clearly implies turning things upside down, and its use is rather figurative when applied to chords. As you will discover in the next section, although the lowest component note of a triad or chord may go 'up' into the harmony in an inversion, the top note does not necessarily go down to the bottom. This is because triads (and chords derived from them) are based on three notes and not just two 'top and bottom' elements. But the application of the idea is best approached from the inversion of intervals, which *do* consist of two notes.

Example 17 shows the simple inversion of the notes C and E. In the first interval, the C is below the E. In the second, the C has been moved up above the E.

Example 17

The note names are the same, but we might say that the 'bass' note has changed from C to E. You will also notice that inversion usually changes the size of an interval. There is obviously a bigger pitch difference between E and C on the right of Example 17 than between C and E on the left.

7.2 ROOT POSITIONS AND INVERSIONS

In the analysis of chords (or in the construction of chords from triads), we have from now on to pay attention both to the chord itself (i.e. the constituent notes) and to the choice of bass note. I'll start with the basic definitions.

> When the root of the triad or chord is in the bass, the chord is in **root position**.
> When the third of the triad or chord is in the bass, the chord is in **first inversion**.
> When the fifth of the triad or chord is in the bass, the chord is in **second inversion**[7].

If you have forgotten about 'root, third, fifth' terminology, look back to the beginning of Section 5 of the unit and at Example 11.

For the purposes of analysis, we use lower-case letters a, b and c respectively for root position, first inversion and second inversion. Root positions are so common and straightforward that the 'a' is often omitted, but for the moment it is best to play safe and label your own chords thoroughly!

If, as is very likely, you are feeling fairly confused by all this, the best antidote is to look at some examples. First, see what happens when the principle of inversion is applied to a simple triad, as in the versions of the triad of C major in Example 18.

Example 18

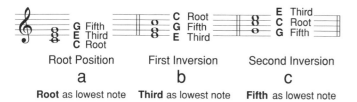

Look carefully at these and compare them. They should clarify the preceding definitions. The principle of inversion in these triads is the same as that in the intervals of Example 17, but obviously the situation is made more complex by the fact that more than two notes are involved. In an interval, if you take the lower note and put it up an octave, the result is another interval. If you take the lowest note of the triad and do the same thing, the result rearranges the three-note pattern. The best way to think of chord inversions, however, is in terms of the lowest note in turn being taken up into the harmony above, as in Example 18.

You will notice from Example 18 that when the triad is inverted the 1–3–5 fingering pattern breaks down, because some of the notes are separated by two white notes rather than just one. You will not be asked to learn specific fingering patterns for triad inversions, though you should be able to work out for yourself how to play the inversions when necessary.

7.3 CHORD INVERSIONS

Once you have grasped the principle, it is not too difficult to recognize and analyse triad inversions. The difficulty comes with bigger chords, where you have to deal with more notes, and with notes spaced more widely. Take the chord in Example 19:

Example 19

To work out what this chord is, you now have to follow two procedures:

1 Identify the names of the notes included in the chord. From that information, discover the generating triad and the *root* of the chord.

2 Look at the *bass* note and decide whether the chord is in root position, first inversion or second inversion.

It's worth reminding you that the top (melody) note of a chord has no effect on the inversion – for the purpose of the analysis, it's just one other note in the chord.

> *Exercise 12*
>
> Work through the two procedures above with the chord in Example 19 and describe it as accurately as you can. The answer is given at the end of the unit.

---

[7] A chord built from the notes of a 3-note triad cannot, of course, have more than two inversions. More complex chords involving combinations of four or more different pitch-names will have more possible inversions.

Discussion

Your path to the answer should have been as follows:

(a) The notes in the chord are A, F, C, F. (I have named them from the bottom upwards, which is a good habit, but you would have ended up with the same collection of note-names, in a different order, if you had worked down from the top.) The note F is doubled, so the three different notes of the triad named upwards, alphabetically, are A, C and F.

A–C–F is not in a root-third-fifth pattern, so the note names need to be re-arranged until they form a triad pattern. (A keyboard may help you here. Try various combinations of A, C and F until you find one that falls into the pattern of

thumb   (miss one)   middle finger   (miss one)   little finger.

Or perhaps you might like to draw the notes in various combinations on the stave until you hit on the pattern of the triad.) When the notes are re-arranged into a triad pattern, they are (from the bottom) F, A, C. So F must be the root of the chord. It is an F major chord. (You could test whether it is major or minor by playing it on the keyboard and listening carefully, perhaps also altering the middle note to experiment with the major/minor effect.)

(b) The root note (F) is not the lowest sounding note in the chord as presented in Example 18. Instead the bass note is A, the third of the triad. So the chord is in first inversion.

You should now repeat Exercise 12. It is very important that you grasp the procedures for analysing chords, and for recognizing triad patterns, root notes, and chord inversions. So please re-read this discussion a few times. On at least one of the re-readings, go through the procedures I have outlined for yourself, slowly and carefully, with keyboard and manuscript paper, even if you had the right answer first time. Mastering of chord analysis now will save a lot of trouble later.

It may still be taking you a little while to adjust to the idea of chord inversions. Always bear in mind the essential two-stage process for describing a chord:

1 Analyse the chord. That is, find the note-names in the chord, re-arrange them into a triad pattern, and identify the root.

2 Look at the bass note to find whether the chord is a root position (root in the bass), first inversion (third in the bass) or second inversion (fifth in the bass).

From now on, you cannot assume that the lowest note will also be the root of the chord. Using the chord at Example 19 as an example, you cannot infer from the bass note (A) that the notes above will form a chord of A. The notes in a chord of A would be A, C, E and the actual notes in the chord are A, C, F. So you always have to work out the names of notes that are in the chord first, and from that work out the identity of the chord itself. Furthermore, if you are 'thinking alphabetically', you cannot assume that the earliest letter in the alphabet will be the root of the chord either.

8   THE BEHAVIOUR OF INVERSIONS

8.1   WHAT DO THEY SOUND LIKE?

As already noted, the bass part plays an important role in our perception of chords and harmony. Chord inversions derive their character from the relationship between the bass note and the other notes of a chord. It is possible to be quite specific about the effect of the bass part on the chord – and therefore about the effect of the inversion itself.

Root-position chords (with the root in the bass). These are stable chords. They may be used quite freely, though too many in succession can become rather uninteresting. The final chord of a piece or section is normally in root position.

First-inversion chords. The third in the bass gives a certain instability, but one that is quite pleasing and useful. First inversions have a 'moving-on' effect, often impelling the bass note up by a step to a new chord.

Second-inversion chords. These are very unstable chords, and their effective uses are very limited. At the present stage in the course, in fact, it is better to avoid second inversions altogether. A few specific (but important) effective uses will be dealt with in later units.

Try out some chords for yourself. Example 20 gives root position, first inversion and second inversion chords of A major. (The one black note here is C♯.)

Example 20

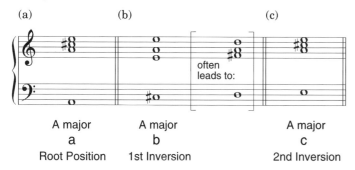

(a)   (b)   (c)

often leads to:

A major
a
Root Position

A major
b
1st Inversion

A major
c
2nd Inversion

Play them on your keyboard, taking plenty of time over each one, and between each one, to savour the characteristic sounds of the chords. Play only the bass note with your left hand, and play the other notes with your right hand. You'll notice that I have kept the same melody note (and of course the same chord, A major) in each case, so that all the changes are concentrated on the effect produced by the different inversions.

 PLAY EXAMPLE 20.

If you think you can manage it, try also to play the chord in brackets, which gives you the 'leading-on' effect from the first inversion. In Example 20(b), it's not too difficult to work out the notes in each chord, and how to move from one chord to the next. If you can pass fluently from one to the other, you will have played your first chord progression, relating one chord to the next.

The music of Example 20 is recorded as audio-cassette Item 8. Use it to check your playing, and to check the aural effect of the inversions.

 CHECK WITH ITEM 8.

Exercise 13

Audio-cassette Item 9 has ten chords, separately identified as (a)–(j). Listen carefully to each chord in turn, stopping the tape after each, and re-playing as often as you need. Then name the chords as root positions, first inversions or second inversions. You may be able to recognize them as such from the overall 'character' of the sound. (You have to allow for the fact that the 'character' of the chord can

also be altered by whether it is major or minor.) Remember that it is the bass note that defines the inversion. It's a good idea to try singing the notes of each chord, and to pitch the bass note in relation to the others. The chords are printed, and named, at the end of the unit.

 LISTEN NOW TO ITEM 9.

Look at the music in the answer to Exercise 13 to see how the notes were arranged. You might also find it helpful to try playing some of the chords yourself. The main point, however, is to use any means to develop your recognition of the difference in sound between root positions, first inversions and second inversions. Listen to Item 9 again after you have had a look at the answer to Exercise 13.

8.2 THE SECOND INVERSION – A DISSONANCE?

Before closing this unit, it's worth just mentioning one final point about the second-inversion chord. It brings us back to our earlier exploration of dissonance and consonance. Obviously the chord of A major is inherently a concord: the notes blend well together, and indeed they are derived from acoustic ratios that *should* sound well together. But the effect of the fifth as the bass note in the second inversion is to make the chord unstable. Although there are not any obviously clashing sounds, the second inversion behaves as a dissonance. You would not normally finish a piece of music on a second inversion, because it seems to need some sort of further resolution.

One of the reasons for the feeling of dissonance about the second inversion is the interval of a fourth between the bass note and one of the notes above (E to A in Example 20c). The second inversion is the only form of the common chord to contain this interval *above the bass* – i.e. the only inversion with the interval of a fourth (or its compounds, 11th, 18th etc.) above the note which is in the bass. (You can check this for yourself in the chords in the answer to Exercise 13.) You may remember from Section 2 that the interval of the 4th is itself rather ambiguous. If you do not hear it as actually sounding dissonant, it is at least an unsatisfactory consonance and most music theorists would class it with the dissonances.

So the interval of the fourth is a dubious consonance, and the second inversion, which is characterized by this interval above the bass, is similarly non-consonant: the same musical or acoustical effect therefore re-appears in a different context. I hope that you will take encouragement from the fact that some apparently simple basic ideas retain or extend their relevance as you move into the greater complexities of the course. Much of the work, particularly in harmony, is cumulative, and relies on your having secured a firm grasp of the basic material.

9   SUMMARY

9.1   THE CHORD

This unit began with some aural exercises in recognizing harmonic rhythms, and in distinguishing consonances from dissonances. If you do not feel entirely confident in these areas (particularly over the matter of harmonic rhythms), you need not worry too much at this stage, because you will have plenty of music to practise on later in the course. It is important, however, that you master the basic technical elements of chord construction and chord analysis that have been presented in this unit, for they are the foundation for subsequent work in harmony. You should be able to carry forward the following essential skills:

To construct triads on any given note, and to recognize them by sound as major or minor. (You could also work out the major/minor difference by counting the semitones in the thirds that make up the triad.)

To add appropriate triads below melody notes.

To construct common chords in four (or more) parts, on the basis of the notes given by the triad.

To distinguish root-position, first-inversion and second-inversion chords aurally, to write such chords accurately and to analyse them in written or printed music. (Here again, the aural skill may be in its early stages but you should be able to deal, in principle, with chord inversions on paper.)

In sum, by now you should be able to write, and to analyse, individual chords based on the triad or common-chord foundation. I conclude with a summary of the principal rules that you have encountered.

9.2   CHECKLIST OF CHORD-MAKING RULES

These are necessarily expressed in the simplest forms at this stage. Some of them will be modified by your musical experience in later units.

- The notes of a common chord contain only the notes of the triad.
- It is undesirable to 'bunch' notes in the lower register.
- Chords should contain the root and the third. The fifth can sometimes be omitted.
- In general, it is best not to double the third of a major triad.
- A note in a melody must be included in the triad that accompanies that note.
- In a root-position chord, the root of the triad must always be in the bass. (When the root and the bass are not identical, you have an inversion.)
- Root-position chords may be used freely, first inversions quite freely, but second inversions only to a limited extent and in specific contexts.

ANSWERS TO EXERCISES

Exercise 1

(a) Chords 3 and 4 are the same harmony – that is, the same chord is repeated.

(b) Chords 7 to 9 suddenly move faster

Exercise 2

See Example 21. Note: The small note is ornamental.

Example 21   The Mistletoe Bough

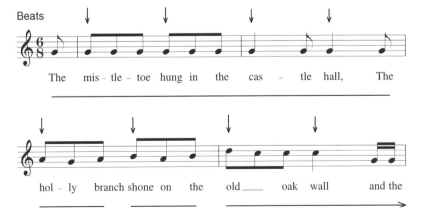

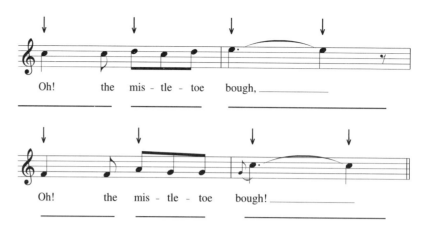

Exercise 3

I hear it as a concord.

Exercise 4

Here are my answers.

(a) D   (d) D

(b) C   (e) C

(c) D   (f) C

Exercise 5

I would describe A as a concord and B as a discord.

Exercise 6

Working from the bottom the notes are C, C, G, C, E, G.

Exercise 7

(a) There are six different pitches, but only three different note-names (C, G, E).

(b) The numbers alongside each note with the same letter name are multiplied by 2 at each octave (1, 2, 4 for C; 3, 6 for G).

(c) The notes become progressively closer together as they go higher. There is a big interval (an octave) between 1 and 2, a smaller interval (a fifth) between 2 and 3, a yet smaller one (a fourth) between 3 and 4, and so on.

You might think that this pattern breaks down with the intervals between notes numbered 4 and 5 and between notes 5 and 6, which are both thirds. In fact, the third between 5 and 6 has a smaller pitch-difference than that between 4 and 5. The latter is a major third and the former a minor third. The difference between major and minor thirds is explained in Section 5.3.

Exercise 8

C	D	E	F	G	A	B
M	m	m	M	M	m	o

The triad on B is neither major nor minor, but 'diminished'. You will meet diminished triads later in the course.

Exercise 9

Mark your triads on the keyboards below (Figure 8).

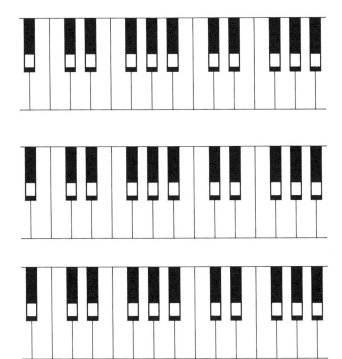

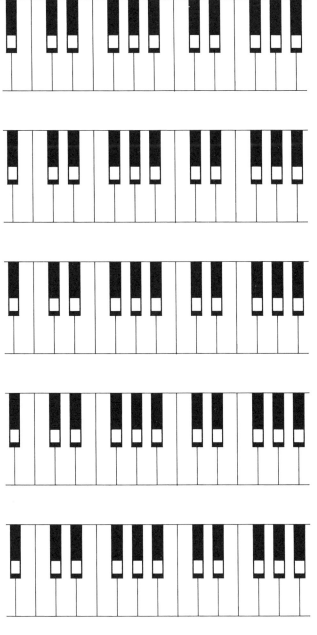

Figure 8

Exercise 10

Triads that will harmonize A are shown in Example 22. Yours might be in a different order.

Example 22

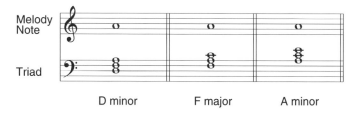

D minor   F major   A minor

Exercise 11

(a) Bad. Correct notes (C, E, G) but poorly spaced, with bunching at the bottom.

(b) Good. Correct notes (G, B, D) and well spaced.

(c) Bad. Notes should be A, C, E, but an F is also included.

(d) Bad. Notes should be D, F, A, but F (third above D) omitted.

(e) Correct, though not very good: spacing bunched at the bottom, and fifth omitted, though this is allowable (full chord is G, B, D, but D is missing).

(f) Spacing not very good, but possible. Correct notes (D, F, A). Third doubled, but this is allowed in a minor chord.

(g) Good. Correct notes (C, E, G), well spaced, though the whole chord is relatively high.

(h) Quite good. Correct notes (F, A, C), and the larger spaces near the bottom, though the gap in the middle is larger than ideal.

(j) Bad. Correct notes (F, A, C) and quite well spaced, but doubled third (A) in a major triad.

(k) Bad. Notes E, G, B (bunched in bass), and wrong note C as well in treble.

(l) Good. Correct notes (A, C, E) and well spaced.

(m) Bad. Notes should be G, B, D, but F and A present as well. (You may nevertheless like the sound of this chord – but it is not a common chord built from a plain triad.)

Exercise 12

F major chord, first inversion (or you might describe this as 'F major, b').

Exercise 13

See Example 23.

Example 23

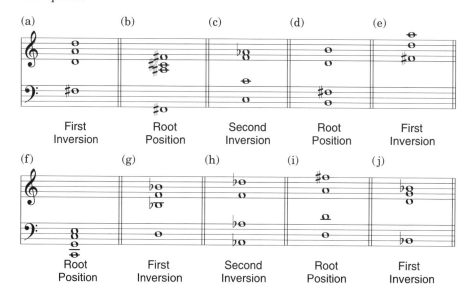

(a) First Inversion   (b) Root Position   (c) Second Inversion   (d) Root Position   (e) First Inversion

(f) Root Position   (g) First Inversion   (h) Second Inversion   (i) Root Position   (j) First Inversion

ACKNOWLEDGEMENT

The Course Team wishes to thank Anthony Halstead (horn), and other members of Hausmusik, for their participation in the video material.

UNIT 6

MODES, SCALES AND KEYS

Prepared for the Course Team by J. Barrie Jones

CONTENTS

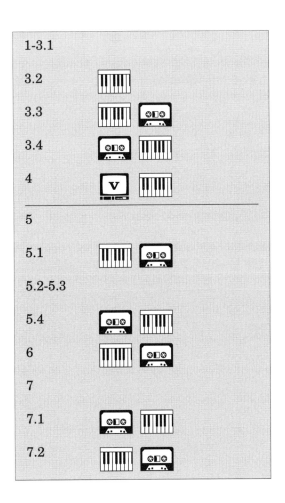

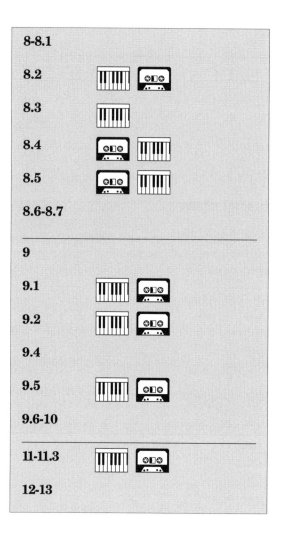

All audio items for this unit are on Audio-cassette 3.

All video items for this unit are on Video-cassette 1.

1 CONTENT AND AIMS

This is a fairly weighty unit. In it I shall be attempting to reinforce your knowledge of modes and scales, as well as bringing to your attention some further musical terminology. It completes your study of intervals, begun in Unit 4, and introduces the concept of the key system. After working through this unit, you should be familiar with the formation of the major and minor scales, and be able to identify intervals. You should also have a reasonably secure knowledge of all major key signatures up to three sharps and flats, along with one minor scale (C minor) in detail.

You may perhaps find that a little of your work on this unit will spread into next week; if so, do not get behind with Unit 7, but try to find a little time over the next month or so to revise Unit 6.

Some of this unit is material you have covered before. If you find that you are now familiar with such material, skim through it quickly so as to give yourself more time with later work that might prove to be more tricky. Conversely, if you need help on some basic problem that may be troubling you, go through the contents lists of earlier units and read the relevant material again. If you feel under pressure at this point, remember that Units 1–6 contain much of the core of this course, and if you master the basic principles in these units you will be well on the road to success.

There will be some historical background in Unit 6, little of which you will be required to remember as part of this week's work. It will, however, be valuable for a complete understanding of many later units, and you should therefore read this material at least once. Later, there will be some reference to this historical background. I shall make it clear which portions of the text are for reference or otherwise.

As usual, you should have a supply of manuscript paper, pencils and an eraser to hand. You will also need to use your audio- and video-cassette players, Audio-cassette 3 and Video-cassette 1, and your keyboard.

2 SOME GENERALITIES

2.1 KEYS AND THEIR SIGNATURES

Keys and signatures are frequently regarded as daunting. Certainly, those numerous sharps and flats that sometimes appear between clef and time signature before the appearance of the first note are not always a welcome sight – even to seasoned musicians. However, you should discover that these essential symbols will soon become a natural part of your notational language. You may remember that I mentioned key signatures in passing in Section 6.2 of Unit 4, and the present unit will consider them in more detail. We shall also deal with keys in a more specific and systematic way than has been done in the course so far.

2.2   KEY: A DEFINITION

It can be instructive to discover how widely dictionary definitions of musical terms can differ. This difference is hardly surprising, since the nature of many musical concepts is such that any single definition is likely to be too simple. Yet these terms must be explained: difficulties experienced, and apparent discrepancies between one authority and another, are often extremely helpful to students and teachers alike. Here, however, I want to refer only to one definition of 'key' in the sense in which we require it for this unit:

> Key (i) (Fr. *clef*; Ger. *Tonart*; It. *tonalità*).
>
> The quality of a musical composition … that causes it to be sensed as gravitating towards a particular note, called the key note or the tonic … One therefore speaks of a piece as being in the key of C major or minor, etc.
>
> (P. Bate, *The New Grove*, Vol. 10, p. 8)

This definition may not be entirely clear to you at this stage. However, I shall elaborate upon it in this unit, concentrating on what has come to be known as the key system.

3   MODES AND SCALES

3.1   SCALE: A DEFINITION

In Section 10.2 of Unit 2 you learnt about the concept of scales. If you play an instrument, the very word probably suggests those tedious hours of assiduous practice during which scales are, with luck, played to perfection. 'Practising one's scales' is indeed a necessary toil for all instrumentalists wishing to master their instrument. In this course, however, scales take on a deeper significance. First, let us retrace our steps a little and consider middle C and the note an octave above. The octave is the natural phenomenon where the

'same' sound occurs on another level, and is characterized by a frequency ratio of 2:1. Within the octave, infinitely many different pitches are possible. For practical reasons, we use a limited number, and even this relatively small number can be assembled in various ways, the resulting series of notes being known as a scale. William Drabkin defines the word 'scale' very concisely and simply:

> A sequence of notes in ascending or descending order of pitch.

and after some slightly tortuous conditions have been laid down, he concludes that:

> a scale, therefore, is usually thought of as having the compass of one or more octaves.
>
> (W. Drabkin, *The New Grove*, Vol. 16, p. 545)

3.2   A STAIRCASE

A scale can be thought of as a musical staircase, as in Figure 1.

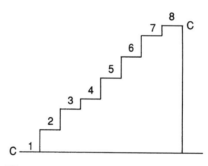

Figure 1

In Figure 1 the bottom and top steps represent the two Cs, respectively, of a scale of C. Go to your keyboard, and play middle C followed by all the white notes up to the C one octave higher.

 PLAY THE NOTES NOW.

You played eight notes altogether, represented by the numbers on the staircase above. (Try singing the scale too.) However, unlike the staircase in a house, the intervening steps of this scale are not equidistant. Those between E and F and between B and C (equivalent to 3–4 and 7–8 on the staircase) are smaller than the others. They are semitones (half-steps) rather than tones (whole-steps). You can see these different sizes of step in the staircase above and in the way in which the black and white notes of the scale are arranged on your keyboard. You played, of course, the scale of C major.

Scales are found in most musical cultures; and there are many different kinds found throughout the world. Different cultures use different types of scale. Some Chinese music uses a pentatonic (5-note) scale, as does a great deal of Scottish folk music. Indian music uses rather different scales. But the two scales basic to most Western music from *c.*1600–1900 are the major scale and the minor scale. Up to this point, most of the music examples in the text have been notated as though they were in the key of C major, with any necessary accidentals (for the black notes) put against the notes themselves. We shall soon start to replace these accidentals with key signatures at the beginning of the stave. These are the symbols of ♯ and ♭, which you have already met on a number of occasions in the course. They tell us the black notes we need for the various keys. Before going into the major scale in some detail, however, let me sketch in some background information on other types of scales. **Sections 3.3 and 3.4 are partly for reference and are intended as an aid to understanding the historical development of scales. You will need to remember some facts, and I have indicated which they are. You will, however, find that subsequent material in the course will make more sense if you read through these paragraphs carefully.**

3.3 THE GREEKS

The ancient Greeks were among the first to name and codify the early scales. As you recall from Section 3 of Unit 4, they called them *modes*. It so happens that it is possible to reproduce an approximation of many Greek modes on our modern keyboard.

At your keyboard, choose any white note. Play it, and then proceed up seven notes until you hit the note one octave above your first note. If using your right hand, remember to start with the thumb, passing it under the first two fingers so that it is ready to play the fourth note.

 PLAY THE NOTES NOW.

You have just played a Greek mode, although it is indeed an approximation since the ancient Greeks did not use our modern system of tuning, in which the octave is divided into twelve equal steps (semitones, in fact). (This system is known as equal temperament.[1])

In the mode you played above, wherever you decided to start from, the general pattern of seven adjacent notes will have comprised your mode. What patterns are possible, and what modes do they represent? Example 1 is the familiar scale of C major.

Example 1

This particular scale was known to the Greeks, but it was one they did not use very often. They called it the *Ionian mode*. It is, in fact, identical to our most common scale, the major scale – allowing for a modern system of tuning. It has a characteristic flavour possessed by no other scale, owing to its special placings of certain notes. What these placings are I shall discuss below, but first I want to consider some other modes and scales. You will have noticed that in this subsection I appear to be using the words *mode* and *scale* indiscriminately. It is sometimes difficult to decide which word to use, though I hope my argument will be a little clearer by the end of Section 3. When referring to the scales used by the ancient Greeks and by Renaissance composers, mode is the word to choose. When you want to refer to a major scale starting on C as used in later music, then 'C major scale' is almost always the term to use; using the term 'Ionian mode', though not incorrect, would be as quaint as referring to a radio as a wireless.

Modes based on modified forms of other Greek modes were still in use in western Europe as late as the seventeenth century.

The first seven notes in Example 1 above can each be used as the starting point of a fresh mode. Those seven white notes are thus used in all the modes. All that differs is the starting point. The eighth note, of course, brings you back to the first, an octave higher.

---

[1] I simplify the present situation slightly, since in 'authentic' performances and in certain other situations, different tuning systems are often used, but 'twelve semitones to the octave' is standard, to most intents and purposes. You have already played this 12-note scale earlier in the course, and it will be discussed again on the video for this unit.

Exercise

Write out the other six modes, starting on D, and so on up to B.

Answer

Example 2 shows the other six modes.

Example 2

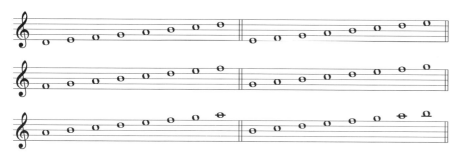

The names given to the modes above are as follows:

Mode starting on D	Dorian
Mode starting on E	Phrygian
Mode starting on F	Lydian
Mode starting on G	Mixolydian
Mode starting on A	Aeolian
Mode starting on B	Locrian

And we already know:

Mode starting on C	Ionian

As it happens, the Greeks gave different names to these modes.

No doubt all of the foregoing looks extremely forbidding. However, for all practical purposes you can disregard the Locrian mode: it is purely theoretical. And the modern term 'major scale' covers the Ionian mode (Example 1). That leaves five other modes, and it would be useful if you could remember the three most frequently encountered. These are the Dorian, Lydian and Aeolian. Two of these, you will notice, begin with the letter that is identical

to the note on which the mode commences, which may help you to remember their names. Some music we shall be studying later in the course uses modal techniques, which is why you should know the commoner modes. We might, for example, say that 'bars 33–40 of this movement are based on the Lydian mode'.

Try playing these modes on your keyboard. All seven, starting with the Dorian, are on the cassette as Items 1–7. Listen to each one, then play it on your keyboard.

 LISTEN NOW TO ITEMS 1 TO 7 AND PLAY THE MODES YOURSELF.

3.4 MODAL MUSIC

Most Mediaeval and Renaissance music was based on the first five of the modes listed under Example 2. Many folk songs are also modal. How does the actual sound of a modal piece differ from one using the modern major scale? This is a difficult question, and one where you need to listen hard. In Unit 4, Section 2, I discussed briefly the type of polyphonic music found in the sixteenth century, where several lines of melody are often heard simultaneously This style of writing, as you know, is called *polyphony*. These individual melodic lines were, in one sense, more important than the vertical combinations of those lines, that is, the chords formed by the sounding together of two or more parts. In fact, modality is not so much a harmonic concept but more a question of the disposition of tones and semitones in the individual lines that in combination create the polyphony. Listen again to the first part of the *Kyrie eleison* from Palestrina's *Missa Aeterna Christi Munera*. It is repeated here as Item 8.

 LISTEN NOW TO ITEM 8.

Composers such as Palestrina tended to think primarily in linear terms, although naturally they were conscious of the resulting chord structures. To return to the modes you wrote and played at the end of Section 3.3, they are all slightly different from each other. Only one, that commencing on C, can be represented by our staircase in Figure 1. All the others start from a different note, so that although the order of tones and semitones is the same in all of them, the tones and semitones come at different points in each mode. If you look at Example 2 you can see that the Phrygian and Locrian modes begin with a semitone, whereas the others start with a tone. (Test this observation at your keyboard if you like.)

 PLAY THE MODES IF YOU WISH.

Thus, to repeat: modality is not so much bound up with harmony as with the disposition of the tones and semitones. It is the relationship between the notes, according to the mode used, that gives each mode its own particular flavour.

The 'flavouring' in question is related most of all, perhaps, to the seventh note of the mode. Later in the course you will see that this note carries certain implications which affect many crucial decisions that have to be taken, in particular over such matters as harmony and melody. For example,

the seventh note often needs to rise up to the key note. This need is not so apparent in Renaissance music. However, towards the end of the sixteenth century, a greater interest in harmony (and thus in harmonic progressions) and the rise of new formal structures in music resulted in the challenging of the modal system by what in effect was our modern system of scales. Although melody was still an important component of music, from the earlier part of the seventeenth century onwards harmony became an equal partner. This new phenomenon marked the beginning of the Baroque era, which as a whole spans the period $c.1600$ to 1750. Throughout this time, the modes continued to exert some influence on music but that influence slowly declined. For example, although some of the melodies of Henry Purcell (1659–95) are as firmly based on the major scale as any tune by Mozart or Beethoven, some of his very early viol fantasias are modal in flavour.

These different types of melodies will be apparent to you in different movements of Purcell's *Dido and Aeneas*. Items 9 and 10 on the cassette contain the Sailors' Dance from *Dido and Aeneas* and the opening of the Fantasia in

Figure 2 A consort of viols (the Rose Consort). The viol family of instruments was a precursor of the modern violin family, although the two families co-existed for much of the seventeenth century.

Figure 3 Henry Purcell (1659–95), by or after John Closterman. National Portrait Gallery, London.

Four Parts, No.1. The former is based firmly on the major scale; the latter is strongly modal in colouring. Can you hear that there is a difference? The viol piece sounds more 'old-fashioned' than the dance, and not only on account of the sound.

 LISTEN NOW TO ITEMS 9 AND 10.

4 THE MAJOR SCALE

 **VIDEO NOTES
UNIT 6, VIDEO SECTION 1**

Introduction

In this video section you will be shown the characteristic pattern of intervals of the major scale.

The notes below in the Summary are mainly intended for revision.

 NOW WATCH THE VIDEO SECTION.
YOU WILL ALSO NEED YOUR KEYBOARD.

During the video section

When you are asked to stop the tape, play the scale of C major on your keyboard. The fingering is given in Video Example 1 in the Summary. Concentrate on the pattern of tones and semitones.

Summary

The construction of the twelve-note scale (every interval a semitone) is relatively obvious; this scale is called the chromatic scale. Video Example 1, however, illustrates the C major scale, with the right-hand fingering.

Video Example 1

The major scale uses only seven of the twelve notes of the chromatic scale, arranged in a systematized order of tones and semitones. The pattern is:

T T S T T T S

and, as you can see in Video Example 2, the semitones occur between the third and fourth notes and between the seventh and eighth notes:

Video Example 2

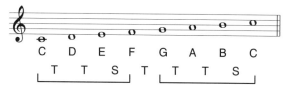

The eighth note (C) is, of course, the start of the next octave, where the scale recommences. The special flavour of the major scale is achieved by this arrangement of tones and semitones. Try to remember this sequence. Alternatively, assuming the key of C major, think of the scale in two halves, C–F and G–C, each consisting of T T S, with a T between the F and G. The two halves (tetrachords to use the technical term) match exactly.

All major scales use this T S pattern, but once you move away from C major you will need to use accidentals.

Video Example 3

Video Example 3, consisting of the first three notes of *Suo-Gân* in D major, needs two tones in succession, and so the F needs to be sharpened in order to avoid the semitone which would otherwise result between the E and the F. This move away from C major raises the necessity for accidentals and key signatures, which we shall deal with in Section 8. It is also covered in Television Programme 2.

5 SOME REVISION AND FURTHER MUSICAL TERMINOLOGY

5.1 SECONDS AND THIRDS

In the first video section of Unit 4 and on Audio-cassette 2, Items 6–8, I discussed with you the concept of intervals. Intervals are the aural (and written) pitch-distance between any two notes. I pointed out that describing an interval as a 'second', 'third', etc. was something of a simplification, since there is more than one interval of each kind. As you know, when calculating the size of an interval you have to count the lower note as 1. Thus, the distance from D to E is a second, as is that from E to F. However, the interval from D to E is a tone, whereas E to F is a semitone. We distinguish between these two types of second by describing the whole tone as a *major* second, while the semitone is a *minor* second. Similarly, the interval from C to E is a distance of two tones, whereas that from D to F is only one tone and one semitone, i.e. it is a semitone smaller. Hence, the first interval is called a major (larger) third, the second a minor (smaller) third. From this we can formulate a straightforward rule:

> Two tones = a major third (or 4 semitones).
> A tone plus a semitone (or vice versa) = a minor third (or 3 semitones).

Alternatively, you may find this easier to remember:

> Minor thirds are a semitone less than major thirds.

Note that even in the major scale there are intervals that turn out to be minor and others that are major. This is because the major scale consists, not of a number of equal steps, but of a combination of large and small steps: tones and semitones. By the way, the terms 'tone' and 'major second' mean the same thing and either is acceptable. Similarly with semitone and minor second. With intervals larger than a tone, however, there is only one way to describe them. The correct name for a major third is a major third; 'two tones' is theoretically correct, but in practice is likely to suggest two separate intervals, each of one tone.

For the moment, I want to defer consideration of the intervals of the fourth, fifth, sixth and seventh until later in the unit.

Exercise

 Play the intervals in Example 3 on your keyboard, then name them, using terms such as major third, minor second, and so on. Count up the steps between the notes of each to aid your calculations.

Example 3

Answer

(a) major second
(b) minor third
(c) major third
(d) minor second
(e) minor third
(f) major third

These intervals are recorded as Item 11. Listen carefully to the difference between a major third and a minor third as a way of improving your aural skills, and try to identify your own seconds and thirds as you play them at the keyboard. Sing them if you can. Item 18, which you will listen to later, will give you some practice in identifying intervals by ear.

LISTEN NOW TO ITEM 11.

5.2 TONIC SOL-FA

This subsection is for your interest and, apart from the tonic sol-fa names, need not be learnt. We need to name individual degrees of the scale in such a way that the resulting nomenclature will apply equally to all seven-note scales, and not just to that of C major. Of course, it is perfectly possible to talk about the 'fourth degree of the scale', 'the fifth note of the scale', and so on. Many people indeed do just this, although there are reasons why this is not really satisfactory. One solution, less familiar than it used to be, but one that you might know, is to use the 'tonic sol-fa' method. Here, the first note of the scale is named *doh*, the second *ray*, then proceeding through *me, fah, soh, lah, te* and finally *doh* again, where the scale recommences. In essentials, this system goes back centuries, but the idea of using a 'movable' *doh* (i.e. one that can represent the first note of any major scale) was pioneered by John Curwen (1816–80), the Victorian music educationalist. He based it on the more rigid French system where *doh* was 'fixed' to the note C. If you saw *The Sound of Music*, you might recall the song sung by Julie Andrews that begins:

'Doe, a deer, a female deer'

She sang it as a mnemonic aid to the children of the von Trapp family, to whom she was teaching the intricacies of musical notation. Tonic sol-fa is fine up to a point, but it can become rather complicated once accidentals are introduced into the system, and it is quite inadequate when studying harmony.

5.3 AN ALTERNATIVE

There is, as it happens, a better solution: better in the sense that, like musical notation itself, it is an extensible system. It uses technical names that can, if needed, cover more than one musical context or situation. This system is the one where each degree of the scale possesses its own recognizable name. The name applies to the equivalent note in all major and minor scales. Example 4 is the C major scale again, with these technical names, two of which you met in Unit 4.

Example 4

tonic supertonic mediant subdominant dominant submediant leading-note tonic

Table 1 gives the sol-fa equivalents of these technical names.

Table 1

Degree	Sol-fa	Technical names
1	*doh*	tonic
2	*ray*	supertonic
3	*me*	mediant
4	*fah*	subdominant
5	*soh*	dominant
6	*lah*	submediant
7	*te*	leading-note
8/1	*doh*	tonic

If Julie Andrews were teaching this system, she might well sing something of the order of 'Tonic puts in a fizz in gin'; 'supertonic' could be construed as a double measure of alcohol. This may seem frivolous, but you should memorize these technical names in the last column above, and you might well invent a mnemonic system of your own that will lead to that end. Certainly, from this point onwards we shall be using these technical names in the course.

5.4 PRIMARY TRIADS

The important point about this system of tonic, supertonic, etc., is that these names apply to the degrees of all major and minor scales. Moreover, these terms are also applicable in a harmonic context. For example, we might say that a certain piece of music 'begins with a long passage of dominant harmony before tonic harmony is established at bar 17'. This indicates that the first 16 bars are built on a chord based on the fifth degree of the scale, after which (at bar 17) the music moves to the chord based on the first note of the scale. Clearly, the latter is much more cumbersome. Incidentally, the description refers to the opening of Beethoven's Ninth Symphony.

Exercise

In Unit 5, you met the word 'triad'. In Unit 7 you will be studying what are known as the three primary triads. Drawing on Unit 5, and looking at the technical names of the degrees of the scale in Table 1, can you hazard a guess as to which three triads might be described as primary?

Answer and discussion

There will probably be a certain amount of guesswork in your answer. But I imagine you included the tonic as one of the three, since much of the course so far has emphasized the importance of this degree of the scale.

The name 'dominant' indicates the importance of the fifth degree of the scale. Dominant harmony followed by tonic harmony is all-pervasive throughout the history of recent Western music. Item 12 on your audio-cassette includes an example of these two chords.

 LISTEN NOW TO ITEM 12.

This harmonic progression has become impressed upon our subconscious as one of the commonest and most effective ways of ending a piece. It is known as a perfect cadence. (Compare this with the 'melodic' perfect cadence in Unit 4, Section 5.)

Finally, the subdominant, meaning 'under the dominant', or the fourth degree. This also has a strong relationship to the tonic, because the latter is the 'dominant' of it.

The way in which these progressions work will be covered in Unit 7. For the moment, just accept that *the tonic, dominant and subdominant chords form the basis of any study of elementary harmony.*

Don't worry too much if you failed to supply most of the foregoing information. You might have thought that 'leading-note' sounds important. It is an essential constituent of the dominant chord, and there is an instinctive feeling that melodically the note should rise one step to the tonic. As Julie Andrews reminds us in the song quoted earlier:

Example 5

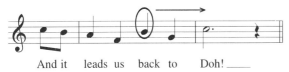

And it   leads   us   back   to   Doh! ___

Example 5 is Item 13 on the audio-cassette. Listen carefully to the way the ringed B rises inevitably to the final C, despite the intervening G.

 LISTEN NOW TO ITEM 13.

Try playing Example 5 yourself, stopping after the penultimate note (G), and notice how odd the music sounds until you complete it by the final C.

 PLAY EXAMPLE 5 PAUSING BEFORE THE LAST NOTE.

6 FURTHER INTERVALS (I): THE FOURTH AND FIFTH

In Section 5 I considered the intervals of the second and third, and we saw that they could be either minor or major according to the number of tones and/or semitones in each. I now want to go on to two further intervals in the major scale, shown in Example 6.

Example 6

4th   5th

Teachers of harmony have different methods of teaching the recognition of intervals, and by any reckoning the methods tend to be illogical and confusing. Unfortunately, this is one area where you will have to choose a method you feel suits you best, or perhaps a combination of methods. Your tutor will have a view, no doubt. Try some or all of the following three methods. The first includes an exercise, which you can then try with the other two.

As far as recognition of the fourth and fifth are concerned, the situation is relatively simple. In Example 6 both the fourth and the fifth are known as **perfect**. Do you agree that they both sound very bare and plain?

 PLAY EXAMPLE 6.

Now try playing the two intervals in Example 7. They are both fourths.

Example 7

4th   4th

 PLAY EXAMPLE 7.

By counting up the lines and spaces, you can see that both intervals are fourths. But the second sounds rather different from the first. Can you hear the difference? It also comes on your cassette as Item 14, so listen to this now, then try the two fourths again on your keyboard.

 LISTEN TO ITEM 14, AND PLAY EXAMPLE 7.

Similarly, both intervals in Example 8 are fifths, though they also sound different from each other. This is played as Item 15. Listen to it now, then try the two intervals on your keyboard.

Example 8

5th   5th

 LISTEN TO ITEM 15, AND PLAY EXAMPLE 8.

It is difficult to describe in words the difference in sound between Examples 7(a) and 7(b) and between Examples 8(a) and 8(b). Examples 7(b) and 8(b) are *not* so bare and plain, perhaps, as Examples 7(a) and 8(a).

Exercise

Show how the fourths and fifths of Examples 7 and 8 differ, by calculating their constituent semitones. (Remember that this was how we differentiated between the two types of seconds and thirds.)

Answer

 The intervals at Examples 7(a) and 8(a) are known as a perfect fourth and a perfect fifth respectively. Play them again on your keyboard, counting the semitones. The first consists of five semitones, the second of seven.

The intervals in Examples 7(b) and 8(b), however, are not perfect. I hope that you can hear that they sound rather different, but we can demonstrate mathematically that their constitution is also different. The interval in Example 7(b) consists of six semitones, not five; while that in Example 8(b) consists of six, rather than seven, semitones. These intervals are known as an **augmented fourth** and a **diminished fifth** respectively.

All four intervals of both examples are obviously four or five notes apart, a fact that can be proved simply by counting up the lines and spaces separating them on the stave. It is the fact that the steps between these lines and spaces are sometimes a tone apart, and sometimes a semitone, that makes the immediate calculation of these intervals so difficult. However, in the major scale all fourths and fifths are perfect except for those exemplified by Examples 7(b) and 8(b), which remain the only augmented and diminished intervals in the scale.[2]

A second method, easier, more foolproof, but more mathematical, is simply to remember that an augmented fourth encloses six semitones, compared with five for the perfect. A diminished fifth encloses six semitones, whereas a perfect fifth encloses seven semitones.

The best method of all, but one that requires practice and careful listening, is quite simply to memorize the sounds of the various fourths and fifths. It is really the only sure way to success. (It may also help you to relate the sound of an interval to its visual appearance.)

[2] You may also have spotted, perhaps, that the augmented fourth and diminished fifth are the same interval aurally, one of those curious but explicable anomalies (such as D♯ and E♭ being the same note). Which name is used depends on the harmonic context.

Example 9, for reference purposes only, are all the fourths and fifths, with their appropriate names, that you will find in the key of C major.

Example 9

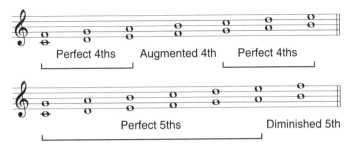

These fourths and fifths are played as Item 16.

 LISTEN NOW TO ITEM 16.

Incidentally, look back at Example 5. Although the augmented fourth from F to B evidently held no terrors for Julie Andrews, I should point out that in vocal writing, especially, one tries not to write augmented intervals. They are awkward to sing, and indeed in the Mediaeval and Renaissance periods, composers avoided writing them completely. Apart from its difficulty for singers, in that God-fearing age the three whole tones that make up the interval – called a *tritone* – were seen as the *diabolus in musica*: the devil in music. You could try singing Example 5 to see how you get on with the tritone there.

TRY SINGING EXAMPLE 5.

Do not worry if all this information seems a lot to take in at once. Persevere, and remember that studying a little and often is the clue to success here. Try to recognize the appearance of these intervals and be aware of their characteristic sounds. By the way, you may have spotted that the minor third and augmented second sound the same aurally, but – like the augmented fourth and diminished fifth – are different intervals.

7 FURTHER INTERVALS (II): THE SIXTH AND SEVENTH

7.1 MAJOR OR MINOR?

As with intervals of a second and a third, the major scale has two types of sixth and seventh: major and minor. Most people can readily distinguish between a major and minor third, and indeed you were asked to do so in Unit 5. The two different types of sixth and seventh are much more difficult to recognize; in particular, the aural difference between the major and minor sixth is a peculiarly subtle one. Example 10 gives all the major and minor sixths and sevenths that occur in the scale of C major.

Example 10

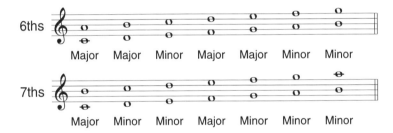

These are played as Item 17.

 LISTEN NOW TO ITEM 17.

Now try them yourself on your keyboard. Listen carefully to them. Do you feel that the major seventh is more dissonant than the minor, and that both sevenths are harsher in sound than either type of sixth?

 PLAY THE INTERVALS IN EXAMPLE 10.

As with the smaller intervals, it is possible to calculate the semitone differences between them. The calculations work out thus:

minor sixth: 8 semitones

major sixth: 9 semitones

minor seventh: 10 semitones

major seventh: 11 semitones

All this appears to smack more of arithmetic than music, and you may well feel that such theoretical discussion seems a long way from 'real music'. Nevertheless I hope you will bear with me, because it will prove to be important and necessary once you begin your detailed study of harmony. Intervals relate to harmony and are relevant to key changes, and to practical matters such as transposing instruments (whose music is notated at a different pitch from the actual sounds). Intervals also relate to numerous other musical skills. Many of these skills depend on a secure harmonic knowledge, which is itself based on a sound understanding of intervals. In practice, you will probably find that 'semitone counting' is a useful check to your aural exercises.

7.2 SOME PRACTICAL WORK

Let us now look at two examples of sixths and sevenths, and see whether we can work out the type of interval each one is. In fact, identifying a seventh is quite easy. You can count up the semitones, as I suggested in Section 7.1, but this is slow and cumbersome, and actually there is a much easier way. First, alter the higher note of the seventh, so that your original interval is now an octave. Then, if your original seventh lies a semitone below the octave, it is a major seventh; if a tone below, it is a minor seventh.

Example 11

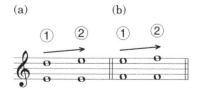

So in Example 11(a) the seventh at 1 changes to an octave at 2. The distance from the D to the E is a tone, and therefore the original seventh was minor.

Similarly, at Example 11(b) the E at 1 is a semitone below the F at 2, and thus the original seventh is major. You can check this by counting up the semitones of the original intervals: Example 11(a) adds up to ten semitones, Example 11(b) to eleven semitones.

Sixths, I admit, are not so easy. You can either count up the semitones between the lower and higher note of a sixth to see whether it is major or minor, or you can try memorizing the order of major and minor sixths in Example 10. (Transposed, these are the same in all major keys, of course.) Or, you can lower the higher note to make a perfect fifth: if you lowered the upper note by a semitone the original sixth was minor; if you lowered it by a tone, the original was major. Eventually, your increasingly sensitive musical ear should indicate whether a sixth is major or minor purely from its sound. Try all these methods. In Example 12 the two intervals, I hope, look like sixths, though Example 12(a) is major and Example 12(b) is minor. Play them on your keyboard.

Example 12

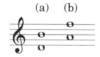

PLAY EXAMPLE 12.

Count up the semitones. Try changing the B of Example 12(a) to a B♭, and the F of Example 12(b) to an F♯, so that the original intervals take on a slightly different character, with major changing to minor and *vice versa*.

PLAY THESE MODIFICATIONS OF EXAMPLE 12.

I have not given examples of these larger intervals on the cassette at this point, although there will be some for you to identify on the next audio-cassette item.

Exercise

Play the intervals of Example 13 on your keyboard. Name the intervals by size alone, e.g. sixth, fifth and so on. Then identify each interval precisely, e.g. major 3rd, etc.

Example 13

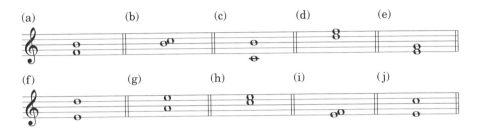

Answers

In the answers below, the words in parenthesis give the precise identification of the intervals.

(a) Fourth (augmented).

(b) Second (minor).

(c) Seventh (major).

(d) Third (minor).

(e) Third (minor).

(f) Seventh (minor).

(g) Fifth (perfect).

(h) Third (major).

(i) Second (minor).

(j) Sixth (minor).

Item 18 contains ten intervals for you to identify: each is described five seconds after it is played, so you will probably need your pause button while you think!

LISTEN NOW TO ITEM 18.

How did you get on? Did you notice that they were the same intervals as in the exercise above? Remember, if you found that exercise hard-going, that aural training cannot be rushed. Keep persevering. Try playing intervals at random on your keyboard, then attempt to identify them as fast as you are able.

8 THE KEY SYSTEM OF MAJOR SCALES

8.1 DIATONIC SCALES

We now return to earth – or, more precisely, back to the scale and key of C major – with something of a bump. I showed you in Video Section 1 how the scale of C major is constructed by means of a systematized order of tones and semitones: T T S T T T S. As you know, a major scale can commence on any note, and its arrangement of tones and semitones is always the same. D major has an identical arrangement of tones and semitones to C major; it just starts one tone higher. When you start a major scale on a note other than C, one or more black notes on the keyboard must be used in order to preserve the major-scale pattern of tone and semitone steps in the scale. In Unit 4 I encouraged you to try out simple tunes in this way on your keyboard, and I hope you have been doing so. Soon, playing ascending and descending scales starting on G, D and F will help to train your ear further: looking carefully at the keyboard as you play, you will be able to see where the tones and semitones occur. At the end of Unit 4 I gave you some melodies which, in order to maintain the tone/semitone pattern for the major scale, required the use of accidentals against the necessary notes on the stave. So on your keyboard you have already been playing melodies that use scales other than that of C major. You can well imagine that as soon as one wants to write complex textures requiring large numbers of accidentals, or indeed to remain in a key other than C for any length of time, a different system is needed so that those sharps or flats used consistently are placed once only at the beginning of the stave, rather than against every note to which they apply. These are key signatures, and I shall take up this point in a moment.

8.2 G MAJOR

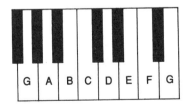

Figure 4

Figure 4 shows a section of keyboard, with the note G as the lowest white note. This will be our tonic. (I have shown the preceding black note too, so as to preserve the shape of the group of those three black notes on the keyboard.) Go to your keyboard and look at this octave now, starting on the G a perfect fifth above middle C. In any major scale, the seventh note must be a semitone below the tonic, and therefore when you start on G, the F beneath it will be the adjacent black note: F sharp, the very first black note in the diagram. Accordingly, we place the symbol ♯ before every F, just as we did in a number of examples in Unit 4.

 PLAY THE SCALE OF G MAJOR SEVERAL TIMES.

If you need to check your efforts, the scale is played for you as Item 19.

 LISTEN TO ITEM 19, IF NECESSARY, TO CHECK YOUR SCALE.

8.3 KEY SIGNATURES

In Sections 3.2 and 8.1 I mentioned key signatures in passing, and it is now time to attempt a definition.

> A key signature is a group of sharps or flats at the start of a piece of music, placed between the clef and the time signature.

As *The New Grove* says:

> The signs affect all notes of the same names as the degrees on which they stand, and thus define the key of the composition.
>
> (S. Sadie (ed.), *The New Grove*, Vol. 10, p. 8)

These sharp or flat signs in effect tell you when to play a black note in keyboard music (or its equivalent on other instruments), and there may be up to seven of them in a key signature. (Sharp and flat signs are never mixed in a key signature.)

The key signature preserves the major-scale pattern, whatever the starting note of the scale. This automatically gives the set of pitches available to a composer working in that scale. Music which uses only those pitches is called **diatonic** (as opposed to chromatic), and the major scale itself, strictly speaking, is called the diatonic major scale.

There is no need to delve into the historical background of key signatures in detail. They existed in the Mediaeval and Renaissance periods, but not in a way that we would consider logical. The musical systems used then were governed by the characteristic properties of the modes, and were substantially different from ours. Sometimes flats appeared as a key signature; sharps rarely appeared until the mid-seventeenth century. Accidentals were placed against individual notes as they arose in the music (much as we have been doing so far in this course) until well into the seventeenth century. However, as musical textures grew more complicated, this pragmatic system proved unable to cope. As a result, to save inserting a sharp or a flat each time such accidentals were needed, a logical system of key signatures arose. As I have said, a key signature is a group of sharps or flats at the beginning of each stave throughout a piece indicating notes that must be systematically sharpened or flattened at every occurrence. The need to add accidentals to these notes is thereby obviated (except when it is necessary to contradict the key signature). The raising or lowering is done once only: at the start of the stave. The system of key signatures is really a shorthand which demands that the performer remember which accidentals to use on a systematic basis. To return to our scale of G major, the sharp is placed in the highest available position on the stave, but it affects all the Fs in the higher and lower octaves too. Example 14 shows the key signature in place.

Example 14

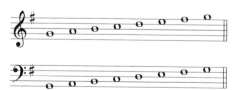

Thus, the ♯ in the signature raises every F in this scale to F♯, the leading note of the G major scale. On a keyboard, this note is the black note below G. You already know that the leading note of *every* major scale must be a semitone below the tonic. A piece of music using the major scale in Example 14 is said to be 'in the key of G major'. Try singing this scale now, and play it again until you can do so fluently.

SING AND PLAY THE SCALE OF G MAJOR.

8.4 TWO FURTHER SCALES AND THE CIRCLE OF FIFTHS

By starting with the key of C major, then adding a ♯ and thereby producing the key of G major, you have made the first step of a long journey which, if carried through to its conclusion, is known as the **circle of fifths**. (C to G is five notes, G to D is five notes, and so on.) If you start from C and go up by fifths twelve times, you will eventually end up on another C, thus 'completing' the circle. The relationships in the circle of fifths will be taken up in later units, but the phenomenon has a particular significance for us at the moment in that when you move through the circle of fifths (C to G to D to A, and so on), an extra sharp is needed for the leading-note of each new scale. As you proceed through the system, that new sharp is retained for the next key. You know already that the note below G must be F♯, and that below D will be C♯, and that below A will be G♯. As you can see, the new leading-note is the new sharp for the next key. Following this principle through, we reach the following two scales and their appropriate key signatures shown in Example 15.

Example 15

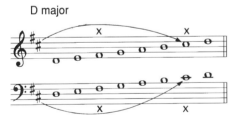

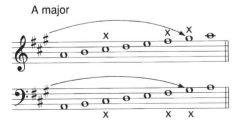

I have marked the necessary black notes with crosses. The scales are recorded for you as Item 20. On the audio-cassette I play just the right hand of each scale, though you should practise both hands.

 LISTEN NOW TO ITEM 20.

Remember that in the right hand you start with your thumb, passing it under the middle finger so that it is ready to play the fourth note of the scale. With the left, the order is 5 4 3 2 1 3 2 1 for the eight notes you need. Insert these fingerings in Example 15, then try playing and singing them, checking your efforts against the cassette.

 PLAY EXAMPLE 15.

The last sharp in the signature always matches the leading note in the major scale. You will learn before too long that this can be a vital note when music moves from one key into another, which from Unit 4, Section 10, you will remember is called modulation. Frequently this change will be from tonic to dominant. Think back to the triads you played in Unit 5. The crucial note is the middle one, the third. You can now see that the third of the dominant chord is the leading-note, as Example 16 shows.

Example 16

When a *dominant* becomes the new *tonic*, the new scale's leading note takes the extra sharp in the key signature. This may seem complicated at this stage, but it should become clear in due course. Note that in a key signature, the sharps (and flats too) are always contained within the stave. You never use leger lines in a key signature. You will probably find it quite easy to memorize the patterns of the various key signatures without too much trouble.

Keep playing the scales of G, D and A major a number of times until your playing is reasonably fluent.

 PLAY THE SCALES OF G, D AND A MAJOR.

For the moment, I shall not venture beyond those key signatures with more than three sharps or flats. All of them are included for reference at the end of this unit, but in fact you will hardly ever need to refer to it. Much of the music in this course will be covered by less awesome key signatures; and music generally avoids the more extreme key signatures. This gives us seven major scales: C major, the three sharp keys of G, D and A major, and three flat keys.

8.5 FLAT KEYS

You will be glad to know that the progression through the flat keys is as logical as is that through the sharp keys, although it is different in some ways. This time I am going to ask you to perform the necessary manoeuvres.

Exercise

Progress downwards by perfect fifths three times from middle C. What are the notes produced? Show your method by musical notation, using the bass clef, but work it out at the keyboard if you wish.

Answer

A descent by perfect fifths produces Example 17.

Example 17

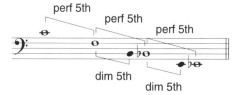

I hope you remembered the flats so as to preserve the correct number of semitones for a perfect fifth. (Failure to include them gives the diminished fifths shown.) If you did not remember them, re-read Section 6 before continuing.

Example 17 showed us that proceeding downwards by perfect fifths from C gives us F, B♭ and E♭. Using your right hand, play major scales starting on each of these notes. Start at the appropriate notes convenient for your right hand; the F a fourth above middle C, the B♭ a seventh above, and the E♭ a third above. Remembering the major scale pattern of

  T T S T T T S,

you will need one, two and three black notes respectively for these scales. (The ideal fingerings are different from the ones used for sharp scales, but for now just concentrate on finding the right notes. I will provide the fingering in a minute.)

 PLAY THE SCALES OF F, B♭ AND E♭ MAJOR.

 CHECK WHAT YOU HAVE PLAYED WITH ITEM 21.

Exercise

(a) Write out the major scales of F, B♭ and E♭ in the treble clef, not using a key signature but writing requisite accidentals in front of the appropriate notes.

(b) In the bass clef, write out each scale without accidentals but with its appropriate key signature. Here you will need to know that, in the bass clef, the first flat in the key signature is placed on the fourth staveline from the top. For the second flat, apply the 'no leger line' rule that I gave you towards the end of Section 8.4. For the third flat, two positions on the stave are theoretically possible, though only one is correct. See which you think looks best in relation to the first two flats.

(c) Comment on the relationship between the last flat in the signature and the same note in the scale.

Answers

(a) Example 18 shows the scales. I have added fingering.

Example 18

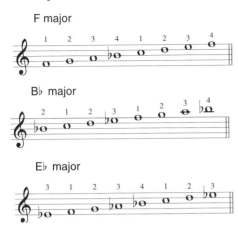

(b) Example 19 shows the scales and their key signatures.

Example 19

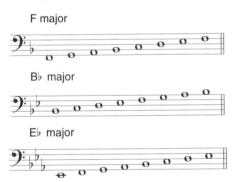

For the key signature of E♭, I am sure you will agree that the last flat looks neater in the lower space rather than on the top line.

(c) The last flat in the signature is the fourth degree of the scale. In addition, it indicates the next flat scale in the cycle. (For example, the single flat (B♭) of F major = the following scale, of B♭.)

Don't worry if this appears intimidating. There is no need to learn it all this week. Study these scales a little each day, play them on your keyboard frequently, and try to form a picture in your mind of the appearances of the various key signatures. If, despite the hints I gave, you positioned your flats

in the wrong octave when compiling your key signatures, try to remember the correct order in both flat and sharp signatures from now on. Actually, Mediaeval and Renaissance composers were fairly casual, and committed apparent solecisms such as this:

Example 20

8.6   SUMMARY OF SHARP AND FLAT KEY SIGNATURES

Having worked through this unit, you should be able to appreciate that Example 20, according to modern conventions, ought to have the E♭ sign in the second space from the top of the stave. Example 21 shows the correct key signatures for the major keys you are most likely to meet in this course.

Example 21

Remember that there is a chart of all key signatures at the end of this unit.

And now that we have discussed the flat signatures, you can see the first stages in the construction of the circle of fifths on both the sharp and the flat sides (Figure 5). At the moment, you will certainly not need to use the more extreme parts of the circle.

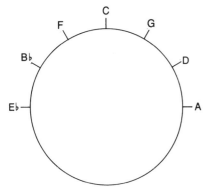

*Figure 5   Part of the circle of fifths.
See p.92 for the complete circle.*

8.7   KEYS AND AESTHETICS

We have covered the major scales and key signatures of C, G, D, A, F, B♭ and E♭. Along with their corresponding minor keys, about which you will learn in a moment, these are the most frequently used, and in fact there will be little need for you to worry about the more distant ones. They look more complicated, but the basic principles of how the signatures arise and are notated proceed on the lines I have indicated. By this stage in your studies, if a piece of music is described as being 'in D major' or 'in E♭ major' you now know what this means.

What about the remaining keys in our major–minor key system? Bach advocated the use of them all, even if his own preferences lay with those keys which venture no further than four sharps or flats. His double collection of 24 Preludes and Fugues for the keyboard, known popularly as 'The Well-Tempered Clavier', demonstrates this. In each collection there is a prelude and fugue for each major and minor key, based on the twelve notes that make up the chromatic scale. In these two collections, it is possible that Bach was demonstrating what he saw as a unique 'character' for each key. This accords with eighteenth-century composers' strong preoccupation both with musical aesthetics and with their specific interest in maintaining a single mood throughout a whole movement. This became known as the principle of *Affekt* or affection. More recent composers exhibit similar traits. César Franck (1822–90), for example, was attracted by the 'spirituality' of keys with large numbers of sharps. Similarly, Olivier Messiaen (1908–92) was almost obsessed by what he saw as the spirituality of F♯ major (six sharps). To suggest that each of the twenty-four keys was imbued with a certain emotional character is only to reiterate what the ancient Greeks had believed to be true concerning the particular qualities of their modes. I should also mention equal temperament here, since one definition of this is 'the equal division of the octave into twelve'. 'Temperament' refers merely to a method of tuning, although it also implies character: in describing a person, one talks about an equable temperament, a vivacious character, a generous nature. Any of these last three nouns can be replaced by either of the other two. The question of whether certain keys have certain non–musical characteristics (as Bach and others believed) has generated a great deal of controversy when applied to music in general. It remains controversial, but you may like to bear it in mind.

We must now, however, turn to the last important area of this week's work: minor scales. As you have seen, there is a major scale for each of the twelve notes of the chromatic scale. (If you think about it, some notes having more than one name, e.g. C♯/D♭, can have more than one major scale constructed on them.) Almost all the music we have been studying has been in the major key. There are also twelve corresponding minor scales. Let us take C major and C minor: the key note, or tonic, is obviously the same for each. But the particular arrangement of tones and semitones is different for the minor, compared with the major scale. It has a different 'flavour'.

9   THE KEY SYSTEMS OF MINOR SCALES

9.1   THE HARMONIC MINOR SCALE

In Unit 5, Section 5.3, you played for yourself major and minor triads on C. Re-read Section 5.3 of that unit if you need to refresh your memory.

To get down to basics, look at Example 22.

Example 22

The first chord is a major triad, the second one a minor triad.

 PLAY THESE TRIADS ON YOUR KEYBOARD.
LISTEN CAREFULLY.

Sing up and down each triad. The second of these triads is the basis of the minor scale that begins on the note C. Like the major, the minor has seven different notes, each adjacent to the next on the lines and spaces of the stave. It also uses the same technical names of tonic, supertonic, and so on, for each degree of the scale. But the arrangement of tones and semitones is not the same as in the major scale. As you already know, the third degree of the scale is flattened from E to E♭ (as in Example 22). And the sixth degree of the scale is also flattened by one semitone. Thus the tone–semitone pattern of the minor scale is

T S T T S (T+S) S,

where (T+S) means 'tone plus semitone', or three semitones.

Exercise

Write an ascending scale of C minor, making sure you place the correct accidentals before the appropriate notes. Under each note write its technical name (tonic, dominant, and so on). Remember that in any major or minor scale you use each letter name once only (apart, of course, from the tonic at both ends.)

Answer

Example 23 shows the minor scale constructed according to the rule above.

Example 23

tonic   supertonic   mediant subdominant dominant submediant leading-note tonic

Now play this scale, starting with the thumb, and then passing the thumb under your first two fingers as soon as is practicable, so that it is ready for the fourth note, the F. The fingering is 1 2 3 1 2 3 4 5 for the whole scale. It is the same fingering as for C major, in fact.

PLAY THE SCALE OF C MINOR.

Notice that the submediant must be A♭, not G♯ (otherwise the note name G would appear twice). This scale is played as Item 22, both ascending and descending. Try it yourself this way too.

  LISTEN NOW TO ITEM 22.

PLAY THE SCALE BOTH ASCENDING AND DESCENDING.

Let us now look closely at the two sections of the scale, bounded by the tonic and dominant. The first section rises from tonic to dominant:

Example 24

and the second completes the journey from dominant up to tonic again:

Example 25

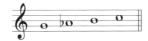

You may remember from Video Section 1 that Example 25 is a tetrachord.

The important and interesting phenomenon about the top section of the scale is its 'polarity'. There is a semitone attraction downwards to the dominant and a semitone attraction upwards to the tonic, as shown below in Example 26.

Example 26

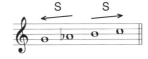

This gives a strong sense of direction towards the two most important landmarks of the scale. The upward movement towards the tonic from B to C is fairly obvious (you have already met this with the major scale, in any case). You can 'feel' the other attraction (towards the dominant) if you play the notes in Example 27.

Example 27

PLAY EXAMPLE 27.

As you will discover, the semitonal pull is, if anything, even stronger when the minor scale pattern is applied to chords rather than to melodies. This basic form of the minor scale is the one that you will use when you need to work out chords in the minor scale. In fact, its correct name is the **harmonic minor scale**. For melodies, we sometimes need to supplement this scale by other forms because, for all its directional benefits, the harmonic minor scale cannot be used in all melodic contexts.

9.2 THE MELODIC MINOR SCALE (1)

Play the C harmonic minor scale in Example 23. Remember that the intervals are:

T S T T S (T+S) S

 PLAY THE C MINOR SCALE IN EXAMPLE 23.

Exercise

Where do you think the problem comes, if this minor scale is to be used for melodies?

Answer

The (T+S) interval near the top is angular, and it is difficult to sing this part of the scale smoothly. (Try singing the complete scale, up and down, and you will find out!) To western ears, the interval gives the scale a slightly Oriental flavour.

In order to avoid the angularity in the top section of the minor scale, variant forms of that portion are used, and the result is known as the **melodic minor scale**. The only complication is that this scale has two different forms, depending on whether the melody is going up or coming down. The complication is fairly easy to deal with, however, if you remember two simple rules:

1 Use tone steps to replace the (T+S) interval.

2 Preserve the semitonal attraction towards the tonic going up, and towards the dominant coming down.

These rules are put into effect to give Examples 29 and 30. Example 28 shows part of the harmonic minor scale for comparison.

Example 28   Harmonic minor scale; upper tetrachord

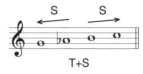

Example 29   Melodic minor (ascending); upper tetrachord

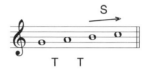

Example 30   Melodic minor (descending); upper tetrachord

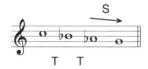

 PLAY EXAMPLES 28, 29 AND 30.

As you can see, the top half of the ascending melodic minor scale (Example 29) is identical to the corresponding tetrachord of the major scale.

Melodic minor scales may now seem somewhat complicated, not to say confusing. So let me repeat this argument and expand it a little. The melodic minor scale has one distinct peculiarity. So far, all the scales we have been considering have taken the same form whether ascending or descending. The melodic minor scale, however, takes a slightly different form when descending, compared with its ascending version. (In other words, the arrangement of tones and semitones is not the same in each direction.) We shall stay with C minor for the moment to keep matters simple.

Exercise

Write out the ascending form of the C melodic minor scale. It may help to remember that it is identical to the C major scale except for that all-important flattened third degree (E♭ rather than E♮).

Answer

Example 31 shows the scale.

Example 31

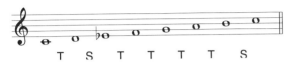

T   S   T   T   T   T   S

 LISTEN TO THE SCALE, PLAYED AS ITEM 23.

A striking difference between the ascending form of the melodic minor scale and the harmonic minor scale is that the large step of three semitones between the sixth and seventh notes of the harmonic minor is reduced by one semitone, becoming T rather than (T+S). You may remember that towards the end of Section 6 I mentioned that in the Renaissance period, composers avoided writing augmented intervals because they were difficult to sing in tune. (They still are, for many people.) In fact, we can regard the melodic minor scale as a practical adaptation of the harmonic minor scale to deal with such difficulties. In Example 32, which is part of a harmonic minor scale, the interval is obviously an interval of a second since the notes are adjacent, but it is neither a minor second (one semitone) nor a major second (one tone), but an augmented second (three semitones). The ascending form of the melodic minor scale thus changes this interval to that in Example 33.

Example 32

Example 33

To summarize: the difference between the harmonic and melodic forms is shown in Example 34.

Example 34

Harmonic minor

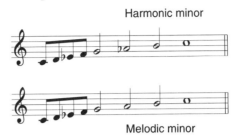

Melodic minor

As you will hear on your audio-cassette in a moment, I skim over the first four notes of the scales so as to make the difference between the two forms of the scale easier to hear.

 LISTEN NOW TO ITEM 24.

 PLAY THE ASCENDING FORM OF THE MELODIC MINOR SCALE SEVERAL TIMES.

Try singing both scales of Example 34 too.

9.3   THE MELODIC MINOR SCALE (2)

Example 35 shows the melodic minor scale in its descending form.

Example 35

T   T   S   T   T   S   T

 PLAY EXAMPLE 35.

 LISTEN TO EXAMPLE 35 PLAYED AS ITEM 25.

When playing this scale with your right hand in its descending form you start with your little finger, followed by all the others, then the thumb on F, and your middle finger on the E♭. As you can see, the sixth and seventh notes are both flattened in the descending form of this scale as, of course, is the third. In fact, both the ascending and descending forms of the melodic minor scale are perfectly logical. When ascending, the 6th and 7th degrees are raised by one semitone. (Thus A♭ becomes A♮.) When descending, the process is reversed, so the naturalized sixth and seventh degrees are flattened.

9.4 MINOR KEY SIGNATURES

Before working through this section, make sure that you are reasonably confident about the material in Sections 9.1 to 9.3, especially the pattern of the minor scale in its variant forms.

The variations in the melodic minor scale between its ascending and descending forms mean that it is not possible to give a single key signature that will cover all possible accidentals that will be needed. Taking C minor as an example, Examples 36 and 37 show the two forms.

Example 36   Harmonic minor

Example 37   Melodic minor

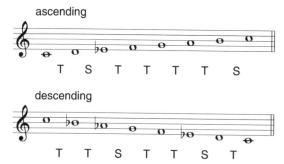

The E♭ is common to all forms of the scale, but the A♭ and B♭ are variable. Sometimes they are needed, sometimes they are not. So, whatever form of key signature you were to choose, some accidentals would be needed during the course of the music itself to modify the As and Bs (with flats or naturals)

as appropriate. Allowing for the fact that you are going to need some accidentals in any case, you could construct a practical key signature for C minor by starting with the following proposition: *the key signature should include all necessary 'flat' notes, counting both scale-forms.* This would give you a key signature with three flats, E, A and B. Re-arranging them in the format we used for key signatures in Section 8 gives us Example 38.

Example 38

You will see that what is produced looks exactly the same as the key signature for E♭ major. This is convenient, as you have a consistent set of accidentals to deal with, rather than having to learn a new pattern. In fact, with any minor scale you use the closest 'major' key signature as a pattern for the accidentals. (This system of minor key signatures is the result of a complex historical development which I have not been able to cover in these few sentences.)

The scales of C minor, with their key signatures, are shown below in Examples 39 and 40.

Example 39

Harmonic

Example 40

Melodic

But this, of course, raises a problem. Up to now you could tell, just by looking at, say, Example 41, that the music was in the key of E♭ major.

Example 41

Now, however, the situation is that any piece of music with that key signature could be in either E♭ major or C minor. You have to look at the music itself for clues as to which key it is in. You could look, for example, at the last note of the tune. (Does it end on C or E flat?) Or you could look for tell-tale appearances of A naturals and B naturals in the melody, which would suggest the use of the melodic minor. These notes reflect the fact that the minor scale has alternatives for its 6th and 7th degrees. For forming both chords and melodic lines, any of these alternatives can be used. One might in fact say that the minor scale is not a single scale but a kind of composite scale with alternatives for notes 6 and 7. The key signature reflects merely the descending form of one version of the scale. Despite their use of pitches that are not in the key signature, both versions of the minor scale are diatonic. To refer to either version as chromatic is incorrect.

9.5 RELATIVE MINOR AND RELATIVE MAJOR

In the preceding subsection you met, almost by accident, a very important fact of musical life. We use the same key signature for E♭ major and C minor because each of them has more notes in common with the other than with any other scale. As you will see before too long, the process of modulation between E♭ major and C minor is a fairly easy one, requiring only one note change (B♭ to B♮) to alter the mode from major to minor. This is shown in Example 42.

Example 42

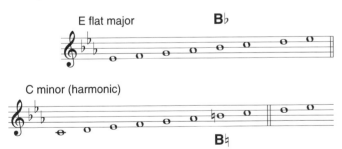

Because the scales of E♭ major and C minor are so closely related, the key of E♭ major is called the **relative major** of C minor; and C minor is called the **relative minor** of E♭ major. Every major key has a relative minor, and every minor key has a relative major. Relative majors and minors always share the same key signature.

Up to now we have related major and minor scales through their tonic note. That is, we have regarded C minor as a modification of C major. In fact, although C minor and C major (say) can be readily contrasted in music, it is easier to *modulate* to the relative key (from C minor to E♭ major) because the two keys have many notes in common.

We have seen that C minor is the relative key of E♭ major, but what is the relative minor of C major? Start by reminding yourself of the sound of the harmonic minor scale by playing Example 43. Remember it has the following structure of tones and semitones:

T S T T S (T+S) S

Example 43

Exercise

 Using only the white notes of the keyboard, play a scale of notes from D to D, then from E to E, F to F etc. up to B to B. Which of these gives you a pattern that is very close to that of the harmonic minor scale?

Answer

The closest note pattern is that from A to A. It gives the following notes, and the following pattern of tones and semitones.

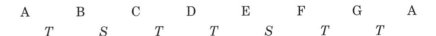

A		B		C		D		E		F		G		A
	T		S		T		T		S		T		T	

The first six notes are absolutely correct for the harmonic minor.

Exercise

In the answer to the last exercise, one note must be changed to create a harmonic minor scale. Which?

Answer

A change is needed at the top. We need an interval of (*T+S*) above F, and an interval of S between G and A. This can be done by altering the G to G♯ thus:

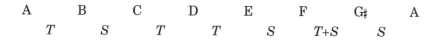

A		B		C		D		E		F		G♯		A
	T		*S*		*T*		*T*		*S*		*T+S*		*S*	

In notation, the harmonic minor scale in the answer to the last exercise is as shown in Example 44.

Example 44

If you managed to work that out, very well done. If not, go back over my answer, following the process with your keyboard. Whether or not you managed the answer for yourself, play the scale of A harmonic minor a few times, ascending and descending. Also check it against Item 26 on the audiocassette.

PLAY THE SCALE IN EXAMPLE 44.

LISTEN TO ITEM 26.

Following our earlier rule, the key signature for A minor will be an open key signature (no sharps or flats), the same as C major. The required G sharps will not be in a key signature, but will be introduced as accidentals. So, if you see an open key signature (no sharps or flats), but a number of G sharps in the melody, then the music will probably be in A minor.

I have been concentrating almost exclusively on C minor in this section. At the end I shall give you all the forms of the harmonic and melodic minor scales having signatures of up to three sharps and flats.

Exercise

You have already written the A harmonic minor scale. Write out the ascending and descending forms of the A melodic minor scale. If necessary, refer to the scale of C melodic minor (Example 40) for guidance.

Answer

Example 45 is the answer.

Example 45

A melodic minor

Check this answer by playing the scale on your keyboard and listening to it on Item 27.

PLAY EXAMPLE 45.

LISTEN TO ITEM 27.

You will notice, if you refer back to Example 2 in Section 3.3, that the descending form of the A melodic minor scale is identical to the Aeolian mode. (This mode, of course, ascends in the same way that it descends, and therefore we see a peculiarly subtle relationship between the Aeolian mode and the A melodic minor scale.)

9.6 SUMMARY

You should try to remember the following points:

1 The harmonic minor scale uses the same seven notes whether ascending or descending. (Example 39.)

2 The melodic minor raises the sixth and seventh degrees when ascending, and lowers them when descending. (Example 40.)

3 Both the harmonic and melodic minor scales are diatonic scales.

4 The tonic triad is identical in both forms of the minor scale, and is, of course, a minor triad.

5 The dominant triad is identical in the harmonic minor and ascending form of the melodic minor scales and is a *major* triad.

6 In the descending form of the melodic minor scale the dominant triad is minor, since the seventh degree of the scale (which is the third of the dominant triad) is flattened.

You already know that A minor and C major share the same key signature, as do C minor and E♭ major. Every major scale shares its key signature with a minor scale, whose key note is always a minor third lower. The minor scale in question is known as the **relative minor**; similarly the major key is called the **relative major** (relative to the minor key it shares its key signature with). Thus the relative minor of F major is D minor, and the relative major of G minor is B♭ major.

When a major and minor scale share the same name and tonic (as C major and C minor do) the relationship is called tonic. C major is the **tonic major** of C minor. For the moment, confine your thinking about the minor scale to one key only, that of C minor, the key of Beethoven's Fifth Symphony.

9.7 GLOSSARY OF SCALES

This section is for reference only. It covers the harmonic and melodic minor scales for all keys up to those with three flats and sharps.

Example 46   A minor (relative major, C)

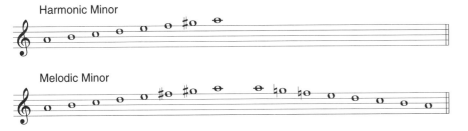

FLAT KEYS

Example 47   D minor (relative major, F)

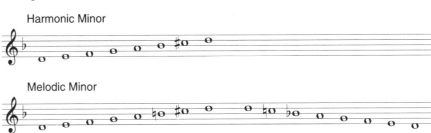

Example 48   G minor (relative major, B♭)

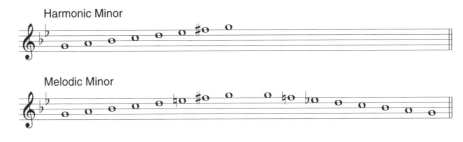

Example 49   C minor (relative major, E♭)

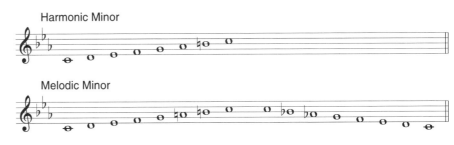

SHARP KEYS

Example 50   E minor (relative major, G)

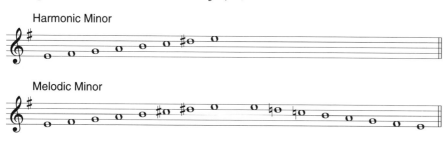

Harmonic Minor

Melodic Minor

Example 51   B minor (relative major, D)

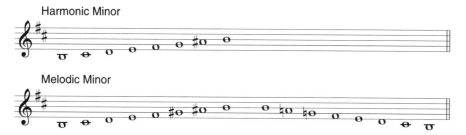

Harmonic Minor

Melodic Minor

Example 52   F♯ minor (relative major, A)

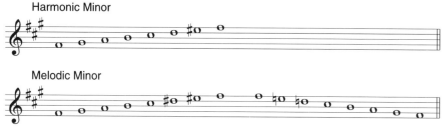

Harmonic Minor

Melodic Minor

Remember once again:

1 **The leading note is always a semitone below the tonic when the scale ascends.**

2 **The leading note can be either a semitone or a tone below the tonic, according to the type of minor scale employed, when the scale descends.**

Or if you prefer patterns of this sort:

Harmonic minor:

ascending →

T S T T S (T+S) S

← descending

Melodic minor:

ascending →

T S T T T T S

T S T T S T T

← descending

Although the scales in Examples 46 to 52 are for reference only, and not to be memorized, you will be surprised at how fluently you can recall these scales and key signatures as you develop your musical knowledge and notational skills.

10   INTERVALS AND THE SCALE

In Section 7 I introduced sixths and sevenths (major and minor) by giving you the number of semitone steps that add up to each interval. Now that you have done a couple of sections that have concentrated on scales, it is appropriate to look back on intervals again and to outline the theoretical framework by which intervals are named.

The major scale is taken as 'standard' for the calculation of diatonic intervals. The lower note of the interval is treated as the tonic for the calculations. Thus

Example 53

major 2nd   major 3rd   major 6th   major 7th

If you lower the upper notes of these intervals by a semitone, minor intervals are produced.

Example 54

minor 2nd   minor 3rd   minor 6th   minor 7th

Notice that these are not simply derived from the minor scale – a minor scale beginning on C, for example, has D (the major second) as its second note.

'Major' and 'minor' here really mean 'larger' and 'smaller' respectively, even though the original source of the description was the major scale. The 'perfect' intervals (fourths, fifths, octaves) are of course common to both major and minor scales in any case.

It is also worth noting that the 'quality' as well as the size of seconds, thirds, sixths and sevenths alters with inversion. For example:

Example 55

major 3rd

when inverted becomes

Example 56

minor 6th

You might be a little surprised about this at first – after all, the notes C and E are both part of the triad of C major. But you have to remember that in Example 56 the lower note (E) is treated as the tonic note. You can work out the notes of the scale of E from the key signature chart at the end of this group of units (p.92). You can see from this that E major has four sharpened notes: F♯, C♯, G♯ and D♯. So the scale of E major has C♯ as its sixth note, and the note a major sixth above E will be C♯. In Example 56 the upper note is C natural, which means that the interval is a semitone smaller, so the result is a minor sixth. You could make Example 56 a smaller pitch-interval by

playing C♭ instead of C. This would make it a *diminished* interval. Or you could make it bigger by widening the interval with E♭ and C♯. This, being one semitone bigger than a major sixth, would produce an *augmented* sixth. Seconds, thirds, sixths and sevenths have four 'sizes', each a semitone from its neighbour. From smallest to largest they are:

diminished		minor		major		augmented
	S		*S*		*S*	

(The letter *S* here indicates a semitone interval.)

As you know from Section 6, fourths and fifths are neither major nor minor, but perfect. Thus, the range of sizes for these intervals is:

diminished		perfect		augmented
	S		*S*	

It is useful to remember this framework for the calculation of intervals, as it gives you a way of cross-checking your results when you have counted an interval by semitones. Remember, always treat the *lower* note as the tonic: the notes of the scale above that will give you a major second, major third, perfect fourth, perfect fifth, major sixth, major seventh, (perfect) octave. If the upper note of the interval doesn't fit the scale, decide whether the upper note is larger or smaller than the major-scale interval, and then refer to the 'sizes' shown above.

11 SOME FINAL REVISION

Some short exercises and keyboard activities follow. Try as many as you have time for. I realize that this week's workload has been particularly heavy. Feel free to return to the whole unit, in particular Section 9.7 and these exercises, at later stages in the course.

11.1 EXERCISES

There are few minor-key exercises in what follows, and they are confined to C minor.

Exercise 1

Write the treble and bass clef key signatures for:

(a) G major

(b) E♭ major

(c) C minor

(d) A major

Exercise 2

Name the major key signatures in Example 57.

Example 57

Exercise 3

Identify precisely the intervals in Example 58.

Example 58

Exercise 4

Identify by their technical names the second, fifth and sixth degrees of the scale.

Exercise 5

Name the three most common modes, (discounting the Ionian), and name the notes on which each begins.

Exercise 6

Name the two forms of the minor scale.

Exercise 7

How do the two forms of the minor scale differ?

Exercise 8

How (if at all) does the dominant triad in minor keys differ from that in major keys?

11.2   ANSWERS

Exercise 1

See Example 59.

Example 59

Exercise 2

(a) F

(b) A

(c) E♭

(d) G

Exercise 3

(a) Perfect fourth.

(b) Minor sixth.

(c) Major second.

(d) Octave.

(e) Minor third.

(f) Major seventh.

Exercise 4

Supertonic, dominant, submediant.

Exercise 5

Dorian (D) Lydian (F), Aeolian (A).

Exercise 6

Harmonic minor, melodic minor.

Exercise 7

Relative to the major scale, the harmonic minor scale flattens the sixth degree (putting an augmented second between sixth and seventh degrees) and is the same ascending and descending. The melodic minor scale has identical sixth and seventh degrees to the major scale on the way up, but flattens them on the way down. (In both scales, of course, the third degree is flattened relative to the major scale.)

Exercise 8

As in major keys, the dominant triad is always a major triad, with one exception: when the triad is constructed on the descending form of the melodic minor scale, the dominant triad is minor.

11.3 KEYBOARD EXERCISES

The following seven melodies, all taken from works in the course, are for you to play at the keyboard. They are played for you on the audio-cassette as Items 28–34.

PLAY EXAMPLES 60 TO 66.

LISTEN TO ITEMS 28 TO 34 AS NECESSARY.

Example 60   Beethoven Fifth Symphony, Finale (Item 28)

Example 61   Beethoven Fifth Symphony, third movement (Item 29)

In Example 62 I have doubled the note lengths to simplify the appearance of the rhythm in bar 4.

Example 62   Schubert, Octet, second movement (Item 30)

Example 63   Schubert, Octet, fifth movement (Item 31)

In bar 5 of Example 64 (that is, the fifth *complete* bar) you will see two miniature semiquavers. They are not semiquavers at all, but grace notes. They should be played as fast as you can manage them just before the second crotchet beat. Because of their speed, grace notes are never included in the rhythmic arithmetic of the bar they appear in. Such notes are also called ornaments. Unit 17 will discuss them further.

Example 64   Tchaikovsky, Serenade, second movement (Item 32)

Example 65   Tchaikovsky, Serenade, fourth movement (Finale) (Item 33)

Allegro con spirito

Example 66   Tchaikovsky, Serenade, third movement (Item 34)

Larghetto elegiaco

12   CHECKLIST

You should aim to be reasonably familiar with the following topics as a result of this week's work.

1   The construction of the major scale.

2   The properties of the modes (and, if possible, the construction of the Dorian, Lydian and Aeolian modes).

3   The construction of the chromatic scale and its relationship to equal temperament.

4   Identification of all intervals and the calculations to be used when doing this.

5   Aural recognition of as many intervals as you can manage.

6   The technical names of the degrees of the scale.

7   Key signatures up to three sharps and flats in major keys.

8   The key signatures of A minor and C minor.

9   The construction of the harmonic and melodic minor scales.

10   The meaning of the terms relative major, relative minor, tonic major and tonic minor.

13   REFERENCES

Bate, P., 'Key' in *The New Grove Dictionary of Music and Musicians*, Macmillan, London, 1980.

Drabkin, W., 'Scale' in *The New Grove Dictionary of Music and Musicians*, Macmillan, London, 1980.

Sadie, S. (ed.), 'Key signature' in *The New Grove Dictionary of Music and Musicians*, Macmillan, London, 1980.

ACKNOWLEDGEMENTS

Figure 3   Reproduced by permission of the Trustees of the National Portrait Gallery, London.

Example 5   © 1959, Williamson Music International, USA. Reproduced by permission of EMI Music Publishing Ltd, London WC2H 0EA.

REFERENCE MATERIAL

INTERVALS

A semitone (= a minor second) is the smallest pitch-step on the keyboard.

A tone (= a major second) is a step of two semitones.

SCALES AND DEGREE NAMES

RULES FOR CHORD MAKING

The notes of a common chord contain only the notes of the triad.

It is undesirable to 'bunch' notes in the lower register.

Chords should contain the root and the third. The fifth can sometimes be omitted.

In general, it is best not to double the third of a major triad.

A note in a melody must be included in the triad that accompanies that note.

In a root-position chord, the root of the triad must always be in the bass. (When the root and the bass are not identical, you have an inversion.)

Root-position chords may be used freely, first inversions quite freely, but second inversions only to a limited extent and in specific contexts.

Key signatures

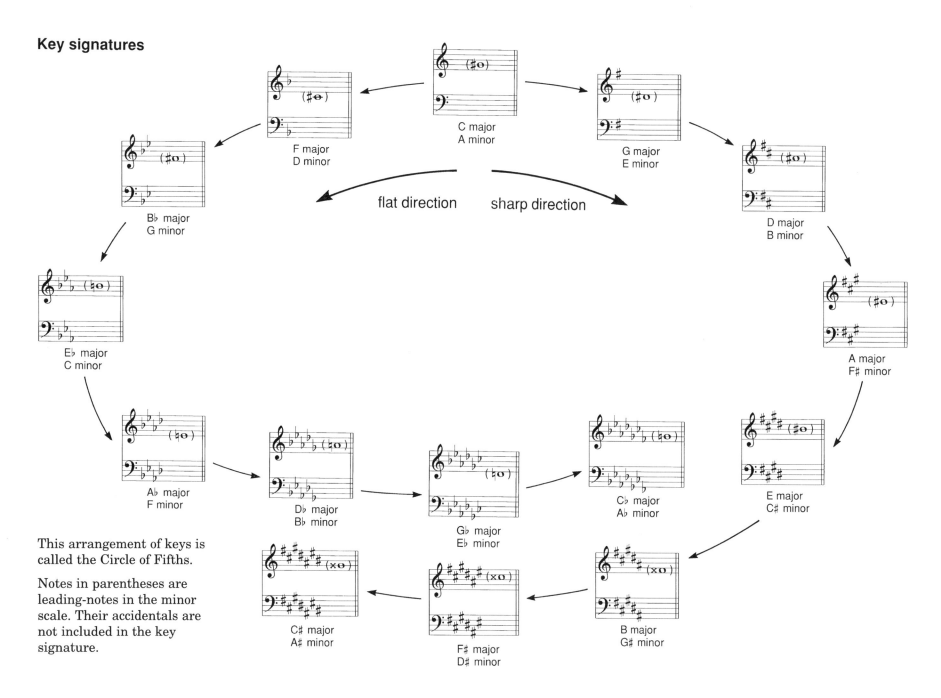

This arrangement of keys is called the Circle of Fifths.

Notes in parentheses are leading-notes in the minor scale. Their accidentals are not included in the key signature.

A214 UNDERSTANDING MUSIC:
ELEMENTS, TECHNIQUES AND STYLES

Unit 1   Introducing rhythm

Unit 2   More about rhythm; Introducing pitch

Unit 3   Starting with staff notation

Unit 4   Melody

Unit 5   Harmony I: The chord

Unit 6   Modes, scales and keys

Unit 7   Primary triads

Unit 8   Cadences

Unit 9   Following a Score I

Unit 10 Formal Principles I

Unit 11 First-inversion chords

Unit 12 Secondary diatonic triads (II, III, VI and VII)

Unit 13 Modulation I

Unit 14 Following a score II

Unit 15 Two-stave reduction

Unit 16 Mostly revision

Unit 17 Harmonizing a melody I

Unit 18 Modulation II

Unit 19 Harmonizing a melody II

Unit 20 Following an orchestral score

Unit 21 Transpositions and reductions

Unit 22 Formal principles II

Unit 23 Baroque style study I

Unit 24 Classical style study I

Unit 25 Some points of style

Unit 26 Baroque style study II

Unit 27 Classical style study II

Unit 28 The Romantic period

Unit 29 Style, history and canon

Unit 30 Baroque style study III

Unit 31 Classical style study III

Unit 32 Towards the examination: Writing about music